ALL
ROME
AND THE VATICAN

300 PHOTOGRAPHS

BB
BONECHI

INDEX

Historical introduction	p.	3
Ara Pacis Augustae	"	63
- *The new display of the Ara Pacis Augustae*	"	63
Aranciera di Villa Borghese	"	71
Arch of Constantine	"	29
Arch of Septimius Severus	"	21
Arch of Titus	"	28
Baptistery of Saint John	"	104
Basilica Aemilia	"	20
Basilica Julia	"	23
Basilica of Maxentius	"	27
Basilica of San Giovanni in Laterano	"	104
Basilica of San Lorenzo fuori le Mura	"	111
Basilica of San Paolo fuori le Mura	"	108
Basilica of San Pietro in Vincoli	"	103
Basilica of San Sebastiano	"	118
Basilica of Santa Croce in Gerusalemme	"	107
Basilica of Santa Maria Maggiore	"	101
Basilica Ulpia	"	17
Baths of Caracalla	"	114
Baths of Diocletian	"	56
Bocca della Verità	"	42
Campo de' Fiori	"	51
Capitoline hill	"	7
- *The Tarpeian Rock and the Capitoline Geese*	"	8
Capitoline Museums	"	9
Castel Sant'Angelo	"	72
Catacombs of Domitilla	"	117
Catacombs of Saint Calixtus	"	116
Catacombs of Saint Sebastiano	"	118
Church of "Domine Quo Vadis?"	"	115
Church of San Carlo alle Quattro Fontane	"	58
Church of Santa Maria d'Aracoeli	"	10
Church of Santa Maria in Cosmedin	"	43
Church of Santa Maria in Trastevere	"	113
Church of Trinità dei Monti	"	60
Circus Maximus	"	41
Colosseum	"	31
- *The Construction of the Colosseum*	"	34
- *The Gladiators*	"	35
- *The Naumachie*	"	32
- *The Spectacles*	"	32
Domus Augustana	"	39
Domus Aurea	"	102
Domus Flavia	"	40
Elephant of Piazza della Minerva	"	53
Etruscan Museum (Villa Giulia)	"	71
EUR	"	119
Fontana della Barcaccia	"	59
Fontana di Trevi	"	55
Fontana del Tritone	"	62
Forum 'Transitorium', see Nerva's Forum		
Galleria Borghese	"	68
- *Renaissance Painting*	"	69
Galleria Nazionale d'Arte Antica	"	62
Galleria Spada	"	50
Goethe Museum	"	65
Imperial Forums	"	15
Isola Tiberina	"	46
Mamertine Prison	"	13
Mausoleum of Augustus	"	64
Michelangelo in Rome	"	84
Monument to Vittorio Emanuele II	"	13
Museo Borghese	"	68
Museo di Palazzo Venezia	p.	11
Museum of the Basilica of Santa Maria Maggiore	"	101
National Museum of Rome	"	57
Nerva's Forum	"	17
Palatine hill	"	39
Palazzo Barberini	"	62
Palazzo dei Conservatori	"	9
Palazzo Nuovo	".	9
Palazzo del Quirinale	"	58
Palazzo Senatorio	"	8
Palazzo Spada	"	50
Palazzo Venezia	"	11
Pantheon	"	52
Pasquino	"	50
Piazza Navona	"	49
Piazza del Popolo	"	65
Piazza del Quirinale	"	58
Piazza di Spagna	"	59
- *Babington's Tea Room*	"	60
Pinacoteca Capitolinai	"	9
Porta San Paolo	"	114
Porticus of Octavia	"	44
Pyramid of Caius Cestius	"	114
Raphael Rooms	"	88
Raphael's Loggia	"	89
Roman Forum	"	19
Saint Peter's Basilica	"	78
Saint Peter's Square	"	78
Scala Santa	"	107
Scalinata di Trinità dei Monti, see Spanish Steps		
Sistine Chapel	"	92
- *Michelangelo in the Sistine Chapel*	"	93
- *The nine episodes of the Genesis on the vault of the Sistine Chapel*	"	94
- *The walls of the Sistine Chapel*	"	97
Spanish Steps	"	60
Synagogue	"	46
- *In the Ghetto*	"	46
Temple of Antoninus and Faustina	"	20
Temple of Castor and Pollux	"	23
Temple of the Divus Julius	"	24
Temple of the Divus Romulus	"	26
Temple of Saturn	"	23
Temple of Venus and Rome	"	29
Temple of Vespasian	"	23
Temple of Vesta	"	24
- *The Vestals*	"	26
Theater of Marcellus	"	45
The three architectural orders	"	23
Tomb of Cecilia Metella	"	119
Trajan's Column	"	16
Trajan's Forum	"	17
Trajan's Markets	"	17
Trastevere	"	113
Trinità dei Monti	"	17
Vatican	"	75
Vatican City	"	75
- *The Swiss Guard*	"	77
- *The figure of the Pope*	"	90
Vatican Grottoes	"	84
Vatican Museums	"	86
Vatican Museums, new entrance	"	87
Vatican Palaces	"	86
Via Appia Antica	"	115
Via Veneto	"	62
Villa Borghese	"	67

Historical introduction

Rome is one of a very few cities in the world that can boast 3000 years of uninterrupted civilization. Variously called Caput mundi, Eternal City, and "capital of the ancient western world and capital of Christendom," legend sets the date of its founding, in a strategic position for trade on the Palatine hill in proximity to the Tiber river and the sea, at 753 BC—but the site has revealed traces of a settlement of farmers/herders from the 14th-10th century BC.

From Enclave on the Tiber to Eternal City

Rome's legendary beginnings were followed by the celebrated period of the seven kings of Rome, during which the primitive village expanded and strengthened. The Roman Republic was established in 509 BC, and with it came the final decline of Etruscan civilization: the city on the Tiber was destined to last. Reinforced during the glorious eras of the Republic and the Empire, with possessions beyond the English Channel, throughout the Mediterranean basin, and as far east as the Persian Gulf, the Eternal City survived the tumultuous period of the barbarian invasions. Rome was reborn in the 15th century ca. and flourished as capital of the Papal States; in 1871, Rome became capital of the united Kingdom of Italy and in 1946 of the Republic of Italy.

The Many Faces of Rome

Even a cursory glance at the city from the Capitoline hill reveals the many faces of this great Mediterranean metropolis, caressed by the winds of the not-far-off sea, and provides an outline of its history. From **archaeological** Rome of the ancient ruins to Rome the papal capital of the striking vistas: the parks inside and beyond the walls, the facades of the **Renaissance** and **Baroque** palaces, the squares that open unexpectedly in the intricate fabric of narrow **medieval** streets. Age-old buildings with shady courtyards and eternally-flowering terraces are host at street level to **coffee shops** and **trattorie** where the daily lives of Rome's citizens intersect the worlds of tourism, politics, art, and cinema, with its glorious capital, **Cinecittà**, Hollywood. In many city **quarters**, like San Lorenzo or Trastevere, framed by the venerable Churches of Santa Maria and Santa Cecilia, and in the **squares** and the **markets**, we

Bronze statue of the Capitoline Wolf *on display in the Palazzo dei Conservatori.*

come face to face with the Rome of the Romans: a warm, hospitable city, the ancient *caput mundi* with its natural cosmopolitan vocation and a great modern city resting on thirty centuries of history. A visit to the **Vatican** will show us the grandeur of the heart of pontifical Rome and artistic treasures of peerless beauty, from Michelangelo's *Pietà* to the Sistine Chapel, the Vatican Museums, Saint Peter's Basilica, and the colonnade in Saint Peter's Square. In the 20th century, the city acquired **new quarters**, some monumental, like the EUR, home of important public institutions and museums, which grew up from 1938 to well after 1950 along the road leading to the sea at Ostia. Not far away is the popular Garbatella district, a garden city built in the 1920s on a hilly site, where fine period homes alternate with the green of trees and gardens.

Ancient Rome

Anyone's first visit to Rome will start from its heart, the **Capitoline**, the most important of the famed seven hills: dear to the Romans as a sacred site in antiquity and later, down through modern times, as the seat of city government, in the form conceived in the 1500s by Michelangelo. The hill offers a sweeping panorama of the city, the valley hosting the **Colosseum** and the facing Palatine hill. The ruins of Rome's forums narrate daily life and business in the Republican and Imperial ages: below the Capitoline is the **Roman Forum**; stretching alongside the hill, the **Imperial Forums**, culminating in Trajan's column and recently the site of new excavations.

At the foot of the hill, near the Tiber, the archaeological area continues with the Theater of Marcellus and through the Porticus of Octavia into the suggestive Ghetto quarter. The **Palatine hill** is the cradle of Roman civilization;

alongside majestic ruins from the Imperial age, the area preserves testimony of the remote origins of the Eternal City. It was in Imperial times—and in particular under the first emperor, Augustus (27 BC - 14 AD)—that ancient Rome achieved its maximum splendor, with baths, temples, colonnades, triumphal arches, and the forums, the largest Roman monumental complex to have come down to us. The common people lived in true multi-story "apartment buildings". The entire city was completely transformed. Wood and brick were replaced by materials destined to survive through the centuries: durable marble and other stones, and in particular *travertine*, are found almost everywhere in Rome, a unifying note that lends the city a special light all its own.

After the glories of the Imperial age, Rome was thrown into the Dark Ages by the barbarian incursions and seemed unaware of the archeological treasures preserved under its surface while livestock grazed on the Capitoline and among the half-buried ruins of the forums. With the rediscovery and the rise of the cult of the classical world, in the 1700s, Rome became a source of inspiration for paintings and prints and a destination of choice for European nobles and artists, who completed their education among the ancient vestiges of the Eternal City; and above all, the city was studied by the archaeologists who laid the foundations for systematic excavations that began in the 19th century and are still evolving.

Medieval Rome
The oldest Roman churches reveal important information about Rome in the Middle Ages. In the 4th century, thanks to the advent of **Christianity**, the city succeeded in ferrying the critical period of the decline of the Empire and the first barbarian invasions. Moving in the direction mapped out by Constantine (emperor from 303 to 327)—who granted Christians freedom to worship and the Roman Catholic church, possession of the city—the new religion consecrated Rome as the seat of its Church and launched it as the new **spiritual guide of the western world**. This function was reinforced when Charlemagne was crowned first emperor of the Holy Roman Empire on Christmas day in the year 800. Testimony to Christian Rome is offered by the so-called **Constantinian basilicas** (*San Giovanni in Laterano, San Pietro in Vaticano, Santa Maria Maggiore, San Paolo fuori le Mura*), of 4th-century origin, and the numerous 5th-century **early Christian churches**, such as *Santa Maria in Trastevere*, although these buildings have come down to us only through long series of restoration work and stylistic revisitations. In the 7th century, the heart of the city was demolished and rebuilt using materials scavenged from the ancient Roman constructions, and the pagan temples—like the *Pantheon*—were transformed into Christian churches. The *cloisters of San Giovanni in Laterano* and *San Paolo fuori le Mura* contain notable examples of an important development in medieval sacred art best represented by the creations of the **Cosmati family**. The Cosmatis were masters in the art of mosaic decoration, which they applied to bishops' thrones, ambones, portals, tortile columns, and floors, using marble and other recovered materials.

The religious buildings of the Communal period are characterized by their Romanesque style. In the field of civil architecture, the **tower-homes** reflected the struggles among noble families for control of the city's various quarters, while a number of ancient Roman buildings were transformed into patrician residences; an outstanding example of this trend is *Palazzo Orsini*, which rose on the ruins of the Theater of Marcellus.

From the Quattrocento to Modern-day Rome
The Capitoline slope opposite that facing on the Roman Forum—the fulcrum of the Classical age—looks toward the Vatican and **monumental Rome**, at the foot of the hill, between Piazza Venezia and Piazza del Popolo, furrowed by the straight line of Via del Corso. Since the early Middle Ages, the history of the city has been indissolubly linked to the history of the pontifical state: with the return of the pope to the Vatican in 1376, following the exile of the papacy to Avignon, Rome once again became a vital crossroads for culture and trade. Stimulated by the now more powerful Church, the city flowered during the 15th century. Rome was reborn mostly at the hand of artists from other regions, in the main from the cradle of the artistic Renaissance, Tuscany. Invited by illuminated pontiffs—among whom Sixtus IV, who commissioned Botticelli, Perugino, Pinturicchio, Signorelli, and Ghirlandaio to produce the *Sistine Chapel* wall frescoes—artists of the caliber of Donatello, Lorenzo Ghiberti, and Leon Battista Alberti flocked to the papal court. "Must sees" from this period are elegant *Palazzo Venezia*, the first great example of Renaissance civil architecture, *Palazzo della Cancelleria*, attributed in part to Bramante, *Santa Maria del Popolo, San Pietro in Montorio*, with Bramante's celebrated Tempietto, and finally what is considered the most sublime expression of 16th-century Roman architecture: *Palazzo Farnese*, by Giuliano da Sangallo the Younger but with additions by Michelangelo. The greatest artistic creations of the Roman Cinquecento date to the reign of Pope Julius II: the *decoration of the ceiling and end wall of the Sistine Chapel*, both by Michelangelo, and the *Raphael Rooms*.

The 17th century saw the triumph of the style that typically connotes the Roman cityscape, the **Baroque**. Caravaggio dominated in the field of painting, while Francesco Borromini and Gianlorenzo Bernini vied for first place in architecture. Borromini created the daring forms of *Sant'Ivo alla Sapienza*, while Bernini designed the solemn *colonnade in Saint Peter's Square* and was an artist of inexhaustible energy in the field of statuary, of which the *Galleria Borghese* contains numerous examples. This was the age of important **urban renovation works** that gave Rome the grandiose aspect for which it is renowned worldwide: from *Saint Peter's Square* to *Piazza Navona*, *Piazza di Spagna* with the *Spanish Steps*, and *Via del Corso*, which cuts through the heart of the monumental city. In Rome's "golden age," from the 15th to the 17th century, the city confirmed the vocation it still professes: Rome is a city more than capable of changing its face without losing its identity, a city in continual evolution, a city that can welcome and integrate all that is new into that stratified cultural terrain that is its great strength and a touchstone of equilibrium and harmony. Proclamation of **Rome as capital** of the Kingdom of Italy (1871) led to further intervention in the heart of the medieval city; the most significant is the thoroughfare composed of Via Nazionale and Corso Vittorio Emanuele that links the railroad terminus with the **Capitoline** and, on the other side of the Tiber, the **Vatican**.

The center of Rome

CAPITOLINE HILL

From the earliest times, the Capitoline hill (or Campidoglio) was the center of the political, social, and religious life of Rome. Its summit is now crowned by Michelangelo's **Piazza del Campidoglio**, defined by illustrious palaces and magnificently decorated with the *statue of Marcus Aurelius* set at the center of the intriguing interplay of ellipses and volutes designed by Michelangelo for the grey pavement of the square. Formerly in Piazza di San Giovanni in Laterano, *Marcus Aurelius* was moved to the Campidoglio in 1538: apparently, Michelangelo had not previously taken the statue into consideration as decoration for the square.

TO VISIT

Capitoline hill p. 7
Capitoline Museums p. 9
Church of Santa Maria
  d'Aracoeli p. 10
Mamertine Prison p. 13
Monument to
  Vittorio Emanuele II p. 13
Museo di Palazzo Venezia p. 11
Palazzo Venezia p. 11

The statues of the two Dioscuri at the top of the monumental staircase that leads up to Piazza del Campidoglio.

THE TARPEIAN ROCK AND THE CAPITOLINE GEESE

It is told how, in 390 BC when the Gauls led by Brennus laid siege to Rome, the Capitoline geese, sacred to Juno who was worshipped here with Jupiter and Minerva (the so-called *Capitoline triad*) were the only animals in the city to have escaped slaughter by the famished citizens. When the Gauls attempted to take the citadel on the Capitoline hill, at the first suspicious noise the geese began to honk and alarmed the former consul Marcus Manlius, leader of the garrison on the hill, who went down in history as the man who saved the Capitol.

The name of the Tarpeian Rock (*rupes Tarpeia*) recalls the myth of Tarpeia, daughter of Spurius Tarpeius, custodian of the citadel on the hill, who opened the gates to the besieging Sabines, believing she would be rewarded with gold and jewels. Instead, on entering the citadel, the Sabines suffocated Tarpeia before throwing her body over the cliff. In ancient Rome, the cruel punishment inflicted on condemned traitors was to be flung from the height to their deaths.

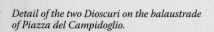
Detail of the two Dioscuri on the balaustrade of Piazza del Campidoglio.

PALAZZO SENATORIO

This building stands on a site on which functions linked to the political life of the city have always been carried on. It was originally that of the *Tabularium*, an impressive building housing the state archives, ordered built in 78 BC. In 1143, work began for construction of a new building on the ruins of the *Tabularium*. In 1160 the college of senators was already meeting in the halls of the new building but the building took on its modern-day look only under Pope Paul III, who charged Michelangelo with redesigning it. The artist direct-

Piazza del Campidoglio with the copy of the equestrian statue of Marcus Aurelius at its center.

ed the work of building the **staircase** personally; it was later decorated by order of Sixtus V with *the statue of the goddess Roma Capitolina*, originally *Minerva*, in the center niche, and those of the *Nile* and the *Tiber* (originally the *Tigris*), brought to the Capitoline from the Baths of Constantine on the Quirinal hill, in those on each side. The work planned by Michelangelo was completed, with some liberties taken, between 1582 and 1605 by Giacomo della Porta, Girolamo Rainaldi, and Martino Longhi the Elder.

CAPITOLINE MUSEUMS

Palazzo dei Conservatori: the original of the bronze equestrian statue of Marcus Aurelius.

The Capitoline Museum complex hosts one of the world's oldest and most prestigious public collections of art. It contains above all statues of the Classical era, some of which are of considerable historical-artistic importance and worldwide fame. Of note among the most recent restructuring work is renovation of the areas of the museum dedicated to the temple of Capitoline Jupiter and the new, light and airy glassed-in area that is now home to the original of the equestrian statue of Marcus Aurelius. The Tabularium leading in to the state archives of the ancient city has also now been opened to the public.

PALAZZO NUOVO

In 1734, Palazzo Nuovo became the first home of the Capitoline Museums. The building houses some of the most interesting examples of Roman statuary, and boasts one of the most complete collections of Imperial portraiture. The so-called **Room of the Emperors** in fact contains *65 busts of Roman emperors* arranged in chronological order around an evocative statue of the *Seated Helena* in which the head of Constantine's mother is set on the body of a 5th-century BC Greek original. Other works on display on the halls of Palazzo Nuovo include the famous *Capitoline Venus*, a Roman copy of a Hellenistic original, the *Wounded Ama-*

zon and the *Dying Galatian*, unearthed in the Horti Sallustiani together with the *Galatian Killing his Wife* which is today in the Palazzo Altemps Museum.

PALAZZO DEI CONSERVATORI AND THE PINACOTECA CAPITOLINA

The original destination of the palace is evident in the splendid Sale dei Conservatori, which are now used as exhibit space for some of the most celebrated of the works in the Capitoline collections: for example, the *Spinario* and the *She-Wolf* (*Lupa Capitolina*), a marvelous bronze from the 5th century BC. The large glassed hall created by covering the Roman Garden is home to suggestive fragments, including the head and one hand, of the *colossal statue of Con-*

Palazzo dei Conservatori: details of the remaining fragments of the colossus of Constantine.

stantine, moved here from the apse of the Basilica of Maxentius. Another emperor, *Marcus Aurelius*, also figures among the masterpieces on display in this exhibition space. The museum as such is housed in the rooms and galleries of one of the wings of the palace, and contains such masterpieces as the *bust of the Emperor Commodus*, the *Esquiline Venus*, the *Warrior Hercules* and the *Punishment of Marsyas*. The **Castellani collection**, which includes many black-and red-figured Greek vases, is a very interesting section of this museum, which continues on into the **Braccio Nuovo** and the **Museo Nuovo**.

The museum itinerary is brought to a close with the **Pinacoteca Capitolina**, established in 1748 in the other wing of

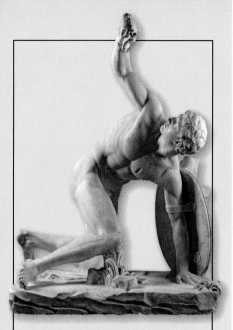

Palazzo Nuovo: torso of Discobolus restored as a wounded gladiator.
The ancient part is a copy of Myron's Discobolus, *while the modern restoration is the work of Pierre-Étienne Monnot (1658-1733).*

the palace by Benedict XIV. His primary intention was to provide a home for the numerous paintings belonging to the *Sacchetti collection* and to that of *Pio di Savoia*. Among the many important works on exhibit here are paintings by Titian, Tintoretto, and Guido Reni, as well as the celebrated *Saint John the Baptist* by Caravaggio. A separate Capitoline Museums exhibition space has been set up in the **former Centrale Montemartini** power plant.

Pinacoteca Capitolina: Caravaggio, Saint John the Baptist *(1602).*

The Church of Santa Maria d'Aracoeli.

CHURCH OF SANTA MARIA D'ARACOELI

Mention of the church is made as early as the 7th century; in the 10th century it became a Benedictine abbey and then passed to the Friars Minor, who saw to its reconstruction around 1320. A place for associative life as well as a place of worship, the church continued in this unique calling into the 16th century: for example, the civic victory ceremony celebrating Marcantonio Colonna's victory at Lepanto (1571) was held here in 1571. In the **interior**, the **Bufalini Chapel**, in the right aisle, contains the *frescoes by Pinturicchio* that are considered his masterpieces.

A view of Palazzo Venezia.

Museo di Palazzo Venezia: Giorgione, Double Portrait *and a 16th-century polychrome wooden statue.*

PALAZZO VENEZIA

In about the mid-15th century, Cardinal Paolo Barbo began work for the construction of his residence. During the pontificate of Paul II Barbo, the building, which had incorporated in its architectural fabric the adjoining **Saint Mark's Basilica**, the facade of which was redesigned by Alberti, underwent considerable modification: the wing which was to become the **Palazzetto Venezia** was added along Via del Plebiscito, and in the interior there was created the famous **Sala del Mappamondo**, probably decorated by Mantegna, which hosted Mussolini's cabinet during the Fascist era. In the early 16th century, Cardinal Lorenzo Cybo enlarged the Pauline layout and made further modifications to it with the creation of the so-called *Cybo Apartment*, which between 1564 and 1797 was home to the cardinals of San Marco. During the same period the palace was the property of the Republic of Venice, which used it as the residence of its ambassadors and further modified the original 15th-century structure. Still further remodeling was carried out during the two centuries that followed, until in 1924, following lengthy restoration of questionable value, the building became a museum and, from 1929 onward, the seat of the Gran Consiglio of the Fascist government.

MONUMENT TO VITTORIO EMANUELE II

Following an extenuating competition, the commission for the monument to the first king of united Italy was entrusted to Giuseppe Sacconi. It was begun in 1885, and finished and inaugurated in 1911. The theme of the building (the "*Vittoriano*") was celebration of the splendor of the nation after the Unification of Italy with the solemn statue of *Rome* standing watch over the **Tomb of the Unknown Soldier**. Note should also be taken of the decidedly classicistic *equestrian statue of Vittorio Emanuele II*, an integral part of the monument, as are the fateful words from the Bulletin of Victory of 4 November 1918 carved in the stone of the last level. The entrance to the **Museo Sacrario delle Bandiere della Marina Militare** is on the left side.

MAMERTINE PRISON

Under the Church of San Giuseppe dei Falegnami, on the slopes of the Capitoline hill north of the Temple of Concord, is the "prison" given the name "Mamertine" in the Middle Ages. A modern entrance leads into a trapezoidal chamber dating to the mid-2nd century BC. A door, now walled up, led into the other rooms of the prison, called *latomie* because they were adapted from the tufa quarries. A circular opening in the pavement of

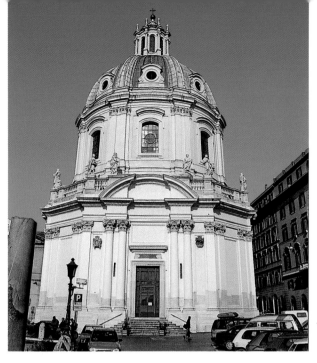

The Church of the Santissimo Nome di Maria.

this room was originally the only entrance to an underground chamber where those condemned to death and enemies of the State were tortured and killed, generally by strangulation. According to later Christian legend, it was here Saint Peter was held a prisoner.

The monument to Vittorio Emanuele II with the Altar to the Fatherland.

The interior of the Mamertine Prison: on the left, the column to which Saint Peter was reputedly chained.

IMPERIAL FORUMS

1) Temple
   of Divus Trajanus
2) Trajan's Column
3) Basilica Ulpia
4) Trajan's Markets
5) Trajan's Forum
6) Forum of Augustus
7) Temple of Mars Ultor
8) Temple of Venus
   Genitrix
9) Caesar's Forum
10) Nerva's Forum
   or Forun Transitorium
11) Forum of Peace

Ancient Rome

IMPERIAL FORUMS

The Imperial Forums were built near the earlier forum of Republican times and were created with the scope of enhancing the prestige of the city and providing the citizens with a place for their markets and one where they could listen to the harangues and participate in religious ceremonies. During the Middle Ages, a minimal portion was recovered and a small residential district came into being among the Roman ruins. Most of the area, however, was invaded by water and became a mud-field, called at the time the "Pantani" ("bogs"): the splendid buildings of Imperial times were destroyed or gravely damaged. Forgotten for centuries, the area was partially urbanized in the Renaissance, but not until the 19th and above all the 20th centuries were the remains of this once magnificent architecture brought to light and the Via dei Fori Imperiali created.

TO VISIT

Church of Santa Maria
  in Cosmedin p. 43
Circus Maximus p. 41
Colosseum p. 31
Imperial Forums p. 15
Isola Tiberina p. 46
Palatine hill p. 39
Porticus of Octavia p. 44
Roman Forum p. 19
Synagogue p. 46
Theater of Marcellus p. 45

An interesting view of Caesar's Forum, one of the Imperial Forums: the piazza had columned porticoes on three sides and at the end was completed by the Temple of Venus Genetrix.

TRAJAN'S COLUMN

The column that stands in Trajan's Forum was dedicated in 113 AD. The Doric *centenaria* (that is, 100 Roman feet or 29.77 meters tall) column is composed of 18 drums of Luni marble. It stands on a high cubic base with four eagles holding garlands at the corners and low relief trophies of stacks of Dacian weapons on three sides. All together, it is almost 40 meters high; the statue of Trajan that once topped it was lost; in 1587 Pope Sixtus V set one of *Saint Peter* in its place. The entrance door to the monument is on its main side facing the Basilica Ulpia. Set above it is a panel supported by two *Victories*, with an inscription celebrating the donation of the column to the emperor by the Senate and the Roman people as an indication of the height of the hill before it was leveled to make way for the new forum. Actually, the column was meant to serve as the tomb of the emperor: the entrance in the base leads, on the left, to an antechamber and then a large room where a golden urn containing Trajan's ashes was kept. From the same entrance, but to the right, is a spiral staircase of 185 steps, cut in the marble, that leads to the top of the column. A continuous frieze, about 200 meters long and varying in height from 90 to 125 centimeters, moves around the shaft of the column like an unrolled *volumen* to represent *Trajan's two victorious Dacian campaigns* of 101-102 and 105-106 AD. The two narrations are separated by a figure of *Victory writing on a shield*. There are more than 2500 figures in the frieze and Trajan appears about 60 times. The relief was originally painted, but the chromatic decoration has survived only in few places. There may also have been painted inscriptions with the names of the places where the action took place. The work is attributed to the so-called "Master of the Feats of Trajan," who may perhaps be identified with Apollodorus of Damascus, the architect of Trajan's Forum.

Trajan's Column, etched with the spiral frieze narrating the exploits of emperor.

*Trajan's Forum with Trajan's Column (on the left)
and the Church of the Santissimo Nome di Maria in the background.*

The hemicycle of Trajan's Markets.

A detail of Nerva's Forum: this was defined by a portico with columns decorated by a trabeation embellished with friezes and by an Attic order.

Trajan's Forum and Basilica Ulpia

This was the most important public work carried out by Trajan and his architect Apollodorus of Damascus, and involved elimination of the ridge between the Capitoline and the Quirinal hills. The impressive complex was built between 106 and 113 AD and was financed by the proceeds of the Dacian war that had just been concluded. The **Basilica Ulpia** is the largest basilica ever built in Rome. It is 170 meters long and almost 60 meters wide, and takes its name from the family name of the emperor.

Trajan's Markets

The construction of Trajan's Forum required the removal of part of the Quirinal hill; the architect, Apollodorus of Damascus (who also built Trajan's Forum), made brilliant use of the cutaway face to realize a unified structural complex which we call Trajan's Markets. Trajan's Markets probably functioned as a sort of wholesale outlet for staple foodstuffs such as grain, oil and wine, managed by the state through imperial personnel who supplied the *negotiatores* of the provinces. Retail sales were probably also conducted at "political" prices inferior to going market prices—and it was probably here that on occasion the emperor distributed foodstuffs to the people (the so-called *congiaria*).

Nerva's Forum or Forum Transitorium

Called "Transitorium" because besides uniting the Forum of Peace and the Forum of Augustus from south to north it was the place of passage between the Suburra district and the Roman Forum. This Forum was completed by Nerva in 97 AD.

1) Temple of Saturn
2) Arch of Septimius Severus
3) Basilica Julia
4) Temple of Augustus
5) Temple of Castor and Pollux
7) Basilica Aemilia
8) Temple of Antoninus and Faustina
9) Temple of Divus Julius
10) Temple of Vesta
12) Basilica of Maxentius
13) Temple of Venus and Rome
14) Arch of Titus
15) Arch of Constantine

ROMAN FORUM

Situated in the depression surrounded by the Palatine, the Capitoline and the Esquiline hills, the area was originally most inhospitable, swampy and unhealthy, until the surprisingly modern reclamation work carried out by king Tarquinius Priscus provided the area with a highly-developed drainage system. Once this complex reclamation work was finished, the Roman Forum became a place for trade and barter. Numerous shops and a large market square were built. An area was also set apart for public ceremonies: it was here that the magistrates were elected, the traditional religious holidays were kept, and those charged with various crimes were judged by a court with all the forensic appurtenances. After various transformations, the Roman Forum became so large as to be considered the secular, religious and commercial center of the city in Augustus' time. With the decline of the Roman Empire, the splendid but venerable structures of the forum were severely damaged during the barbarian invasions, especially those of the Goths (410 AD) and of the Vandals (455 AD). The Roman Forum meanwhile became a place of worship for the early Christians, who built the Churches of Santi Sergio e Bacco (on the Via Sacra), of Sant'Adriano (near the Curia), and of Santi Cosma e Damiano (Temple of Peace). During the Middle Ages, it became a pasture for sheep and cattle (hence its name of "Campo Vaccino"). For many centuries the prestige of the Roman Forum was a thing of the past; not until the early 20th century was the area systematically rehabilitated with excavation campaigns that lasted for decades on end. Thanks to these efforts, much splendid evidence of the Rome of the kings as well as that of the Republic and the Empire has again been brought to light.

View of the Roman Forum: in the foreground, on the left, the Temple of Vespasian, in the centre, the Arch of Septimus Severus and behind it the Church of Santi Luca e Martina; on the right, the Temple of Saturn.

View of the western part of the Roman Forum. Here we can see the Arch of Septimius Severus (above left) next to the Curia (the square brick building), the Temple of Castor and Pollux (in the lower left corner), the Temple of Vesta (the circular structure in the lower middle foreground), the Basilica Aemilia (the ruins next to the Curia), the Temple of Divus Julius (the base can be seen behind the remains of the Temple of Vesta) and the Temple of Antoninus and Faustina (on the right).

Basilica Aemilia

The basilica runs along the entire long side of the square of the Roman Forum and is the only basilica of the republican period still in existence. The basilica as a type is probably of eastern Hellenistic origin; in Rome, these buildings provided a place for carrying on the political, economic and judiciary functions of the forum when the weather made it impossible to proceed in the open air.

Temple of Antoninus and Faustina

The monumental inscription on the architrave identifies this building as the temple of the emperor Antoninus Pius and his wife Faustina. It was originally erected in honor of Faustina alone, by her husband, after her death in 141 AD. When Antoninus Pius also died, in 161 AD, the temple was dedicated to the deified imperial couple by Senate decree.

ARCH OF SEPTIMIUS SEVERUS

The arch is situated between the Rostra and the Curia and closes off the Roman Forum to the northeast. It was built in 203 AD to celebrate the two Parthian campaigns conducted by Septimius Severus in 195 and 197 AD. The arch is about 20 meters high, 25 meters wide and more than 11 meters deep, with three passageways, a large one in the center and two smaller ones at the sides; short flights of steps lead up to each. On top is a tall attic with a monumental inscription dedicating the arch to Septimius Severus and his son Caracalla. Representations of the monument on antique coins show that on the summit there was also once a bronze quadriga with the emperors. On the front are four columns standing on tall plinths, decorated with reliefs of Roman soldiers and Parthian prisoners. The decoration includes two *Victories* above the *Genii of the Seasons* that frame the central opening, and personifications of the major rivers on the side openings; above, a small frieze commemorates the triumphal procession of the emperors. The keystones represent various gods: *Mars* appears twice in the main arch, while two female and two male figures, one of whom is *Hercules*, adorn the lesser arches.

But the most interesting part of the decoration is the series of four panels set above the side openings, in which the most significant episodes of the two Parthian campaigns are narrated.

The south side of the Arch of Septimius Severus.

There are two reasons why the building has reached us in good condition; first, because the **Church of San Lorenzo in Miranda** was built inside it in the early Middle Ages, and secondly because it was unusually solidly built. Interesting fragments of sculpture, which belonged to the cult statues of the imperial couple, have been found near the temple.

The ruins of the colonnade of the Temple of Castor and Pollux with a section of entablature.

A view of the Roman Forum, traversed by the Via Sacra, at dusk. On the left is the Temple of Antoninus and Faustina and next to it the cupola of the Temple of Romulus, which today forms part of the Church of Saints Cosmas and Damian and the remains of the Basilica of Maxentius; in the centre, further back, the Church of Santa Francesca Romana with the Colosseum behind it; on the right the Basilica Julia (below) and the Temple of Vesta.

The remains of the front of the Temple of Saturn and, on the right, the Temple of Vespasian.

THE THREE ARCHITECTURAL ORDERS

Doric order: the column has grooves with sharp edges; it does not have a base and thus rests directly on the floor of the temple. The capital consists of an echinus (the lower part) like a flattened cushion and a square abacus.

Ionic order: the column rests on a base and has grooves separated by flattened fillets. The capital has lateral volutes with a rectangular abacus.

Corinthian order: the column has a base and the fluted grooves have cut edges. The capital is decorated with acanthus leaves and small volutes curving inwards to the column.

BASILICA JULIA

Construction of this immense structure divided into five naves by columns was begun in 54 BC by Caesar. It was completed by Augustus and restored during Diocletian's time.

TEMPLE OF SATURN

It was erected in 497 BC by Titus Tatius on the site of the ancient altar dedicated to Saturn. The eight surviving columns date to the reconstruction of 283 AD.

TEMPLE OF CASTOR AND POLLUX

Inaugurated in 484 BC, this temple was totally rebuilt by Tiberius in the early 1st century AD; the ruins we see today date to that period.

TEMPLE OF VESPASIAN

Built by Domitian in 81 AD in honor of his father Vespasian and his brother Titus. There remain three beautiful Corinthian columns supporting an architrave decorated with friezes showing sacrificial objects.

A view of the House of the vestals with the Church of Santa Francesca Romana in the background.

The remains of the Temple of Divus Julius.

The Temple of Vesta in the typical circular form.

TEMPLE OF THE DIVUS JULIUS

It was built in 29 BC by Augustus, as part of his project for the restructuring of the area of the Roman Forum. The temple, dedicated to the deified Julius Caesar (the first example of such deification in Rome), stands on the site where Caesar's body was cremated before his ashes were taken to the Regia, his official residence as *pontifex maximus*. A marble column was erected here in memory of the "father of the country."

The temple may be said to reflect a true propagandistic effort by the emperor, whose aim was to have the whole forum echo with the name of the *gens Julia*.

TEMPLE OF VESTA

Located to the south of the Via Sacra in front of the Regia, this is one of the oldest temples in Rome, although its present appearance dates to 191 AD when it was restored by Julia Domna, wife of Septimius Severus. The fire sacred to Vesta, the goddess of the household hearth, had to be kept perennially burning in this temple, for disaster threatened if the flame were to go out. But this fact obviously meant that the building was frequently in danger of fire, hence the many restorations. A trapezoidal cavity in the podium, accessible only from the cella, may be the *penus Vestae*; that is, the *sancta sanctorum* of the temple, a sort of storeroom that only the vestal virgins could enter that contained the objects Aeneas was said to have brought back after the destruction of Troy as proof of the universal glory of Rome. These treasures included the *Palladium*, an ancient wooden image of Minerva, and the images of the Penates. The *Atrium Vestae*, on the south side of the Via Sacra, was a complex consisting of the Temple of Vesta and the **House of the vestals**.

The Temple of the Divus Romulus with its original bronze doors.

TEMPLE OF THE DIVUS ROMULUS

This temple, begun by Maxentius and completed by Constantine, has remained practically intact thanks to its having been transformed, in the Middle Ages, into the atrium of the church of Santi Cosma e Damiano; the bronze door is the late Imperial Age original.

The ruins of the Basilica of Maxentius.

BASILICA OF MAXENTIUS

Access to the Basilica of Maxentius, which stands outside the current archaeological area of the Roman Forum, is from the Via dei Fori Imperiali. The building was begun in 308 AD by Maxentius and completed by Constantine, who modified the internal layout by shifting the entrance from the east to the south side on the Via Sacra.

The building occupies an area of 100 by 65 meters and stands on a platform which is in part a superstructure over storerooms of considerable size. The ground plan and dimensions of the building were inspired by the majestic halls of the imperial baths, which were also called "basilicas."

View of the Roman Forum with the Church of Santa Francesca Romana, the Arch of Titus and the Colosseum in the background.

The Arch of Titus, the oldest of the Imperial-age arches in the Roman Forum.

ARCH OF TITUS

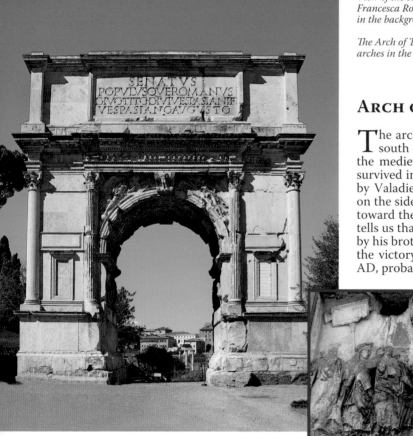

The arch rises in the eastern part of the forums area, south of the Temple of Venus and Roma. As part of the medieval fortifications of the Frangipane family, it survived into the 19th century and in 1822 was restored by Valadier, as recorded in the inscription on the attic on the side facing the forum. The inscription on the side toward the Colosseum is instead coeval with the arch; it tells us that the arch was dedicated to the emperor Titus by his brother and successor Domitian to commemorate the victory of the former in the Judaic campaign of 70 AD, probably after Titus' death in 81 AD.

Detail of the bas-relief on the south side of the Arch of Titus representing the procession of Romans triumphantly carrying the spoils of the Temple of Solomon in Jerusalem. Visible in this detail is the temple's seven-stemmed candelabra.

TEMPLE OF VENUS AND ROME

Hadrian built this enormous temple in 121 AD. To do so he demolished the remains of Nero's Domus Aurea and the gigantic statue of the same emperor that had given the name to the Colosseum.

ARCH OF CONSTANTINE

The largest of the arches erected in Rome, on the route followed by triumphal processions of antiquity between the Caelian and the Palatine hills was built in 315 AD by decree of the Senate and the Roman people to celebrate the 10th anniversary of Constantine's ascent to the throne and his victory over Maxentius in the Battle of the Milvian Bridge in 312.

For decoration of the arch, a number of reliefs and sculptures from other monuments were employed. The most significant part of Constantine's decoration is the large historical frieze above the lesser openings and on the short sides of the arch. The story begins on the western side, with the *Departure of Constan-*

The remains of the colossal Temple of Venus and Roma, built under Hadrian in 121 AD.

tine from Milan. It continues on the south side with the representations of the *Siege of Verona* by Constantine's troops and of the emperor protected by two bodyguards while a *Victory* places a wreath on his head. On the same side is a representation of the *Battle of the Milvian Bridge,* with Constantine on the bridge accompanied by the personification of *Virtus* and a *Victory*, and the *De-*

feat of Maxentius and his troops. The short eastern side presents the *Emperor's triumphal entrance into Rome* on a chariot preceded by Roman foot soldiers and horsemen. On the north side, *Constantine* is shown *addressing the crowd near the Rostra*: he is the only person presented frontally, in accordance with the hieratic concept of sovereignty which had by this time become well established.

The majestic Arch of Constantine.

A view of the exterior of the Colosseum illustrating the four-order construction plan and what remains of the travertine facing.

COLOSSEUM

The largest amphitheater ever built in Rome and the symbol par excellence of Romanism was the work of the Flavian emperors and was for this reason called the *Amphiteatrum Flavium.*

The name "Colosseum" was first used in the Middle Ages and derives from the colossal bronze statue of Nero as sun god which stood on the site of the vestibule of the Domus Aurea, near the amphitheater. Emperor Vespasian began construction of the Colosseum to provide Rome with a large permanent amphitheater in place of the Amphitheater of Taurus in the Campus Martius, a temporary wooden structure, erected by Nero after the fire of 64 AD. Work began in the early years of Vespasian's reign. After Titus had completed the fourth and fifth tiers, the amphitheater was inaugurated in 80 AD,

with magnificent spectacles and games which lasted a hundred days. It assumed its present aspect and size only under Domitian. He added the substructures of the arena. This meant that the *naumachie* (naval battles, for which the arena had to be flooded) could no longer be held in the Colosseum as the literary sources tell us they had previously been. Additional work was carried out by Nerva, Trajan and Antoninus Pius and other emperors. The last attempt at restoration was made by Theodoric king of the Ostragoths; after his time, the building was totally abandoned. It thus became the fortress of the Frangipane family in the Middle Ages. From the 15th through the mid-18th century, the once-great amphitheater was transformed into a simple quarry for blocks of travertine until it was consecrated by Pope Benedict XV.

THE SPECTACLES

Various types of spectacles were held in the Colosseum: the *munera*, or contests between gladiators, the *venationes*, or hunts of wild beasts, and the *naumachie*. Christians may or may not have been sent to their death as martyrs in the Colosseum. A final point to consider is the number of spectators the Colosseum was capable of containing: opinions vary, but the figure must have been around 50,000.

THE NAUMACHIE

The drawing, conserved in the Museo della Civiltà Romana, shows the representation of a naumachia, a spectacle that reproduced a naval battle inside an amphitheater or a building specially built to stage such an event. The *naumachiarii* (the participants in these games, often prisoners sentenced to death, given the cruelty of the spectacles) were divided into two fleets, which often represented maritime powers of antiquity. The first naumachia in the Colosseum took place in 80 AD. It is not clear how amphitheatres were filled with water, although recent research on the foundations of the Colosseum have shed light on a system of channels that were probably used to take water in and out of the arena.

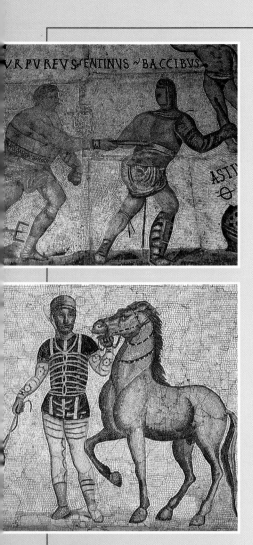

Aerial view of the Colosseum.

Bottom left, Museo Borghese: mosaic representing a fight between a gladiator and a fierce beast coming from Tusculum (second half of the 3rd century AD).

Top, Villa Borghese: a mosaic with scenes of gladiators (3rd-4th cent.) from the Torrenuova estate in the Tusculum area.

Above, Museo Nazionale Romano: the Chariot Race, a floor mosaic lifted from the Villa di Baccano.

THE CONSTRUCTION OF THE COLOSSEUM

The building is **elliptical** in form and measures 188 x 156 meters at the perimeter and 86 x 54 meters inside; it is almost 49 meters in height. The **four-story facade** is built entirely of **travertine**. The three lower stories have 80 arches each, supported by piers and framed by encased three-quarter columns that are Doric on the first level, Ionic on the second, and Corinthian on the third. The **four entrances of honor**, reserved for upper class persons of rank such as magistrates, members of the religious colleges, and the vestal virgins, were situated at the ends of the principal axes of the building and were unnumbered. Inside, the **cavea** was separated from the arena by a podium almost four meters high, behind which the seats of honor were arranged. The cavea was divided in the horizontal sense into three orders (*maeniana*) separated by walls in masonry (*baltei*). The first two maeniana had marble seats and were cut through vertically by the entrance aisles (*vomitoria*) and stairs. The result was to create sectors called *cunei*. The third *maenianum*, or *maenianum summum*, had wooden tiers and was separated from the maenianum secundum below by a high wall. There was a colonnade with a gallery reserved for the women, above which a terrace provided standing room only for the lower classes. The tiers closest to the arena were reserved for senators. The **arena** was originally covered with wooden floorboards which could be removed as required.

Gladiators in the arena. Print from a painting by Jean-Leon Gerome.

Detail of the tribunes of the Colosseum as they appear today.

THE GLADIATORS

The story of the gladiators is a long one that goes back in time to the Etruscan world, where they were key players in funerary rites celebrated to drive off the spirits of the dead. What began as human sacrifice soon turned into combat between prisoners of war, slaves, prisoners sentenced to death, and later even free citizens who sought to capture a moment of glory and celebrity. The phenomenon reached its highest peaks of splendor and greatest diffusion in the Roman world, where the gladiatorial combats were enormously popular—as we see from the huge arenas consecrated to them. The combat lasted an entire day and attracted thousands of spectators. And it was the crowd, these impassioned spectators, who decreed the survival or death of the gladiator defeated after a ferocious, no-holds-barred match: a mass waving of handkerchiefs spared him, especially if he had fought valiantly and intrepidly; otherwise, by turning their thumbs down, the spectators voted for his execution. The crowd's sentence was final: even the emperor, when he attended the games, turned to the crowd to hear their judgment before sparing the gladiator or decreeing his death. But if all went well, the victor was regaled with crowns of laurel, money, honor, and immense glory.

Detail of a mosaic representing a quadriga competing at the Circus Maximus in Rome.

Ancient Rome

PALATINE HILL AND CIRCUS MAXIMUS

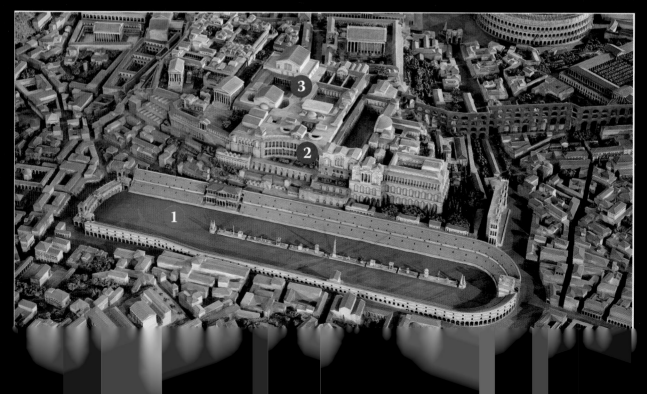

The stadium of the Domus Augustana.

PALATINE HILL

This is the most famous of Rome's hills and it retains the earliest memories of the old city. In fact, it was on the Palatine that the first groups of huts were built, way before the city spread to encompass the adjacent hills. Prominent public buildings, large temples and many private dwellings such as those of Cicero, Crassus and Tiberius Gracchus stood here.

Later on, the hill became the residence of the emperors of Rome and the site of their sumptuous palaces, including the **Domus Augustana**, the **Domus Flavia**, the **Domus Transitoria**, the **Domus Aurea**, and the **Domus Tiberiana**, of which considerable remains are still extant. Later still, the Palatine was the residence of the Gothic kings and of many popes and emperors of the Western Empire; in the Middle Ages convents and churches were built. Finally, in the 16th century, most of the hill was occupied by the immense structures of **Villa Farnese** and the **Horti Farnesiani** (the first real botanical gardens). Archaeological excavations begun on the Palatine in the 18th century brought to light much evidence of Rome's past, including the remains of the Domus Augustana, splendid paintings of Republican period, and the remains of the first dwellings that stood on the hill, not to mention the magnificent 16th-century entrance portal to the Horti Farnesiani.

DOMUS AUGUSTANA

The building of Domitian's grandiose palace on the Palatine gave the hill its definitive topographical disposition and firmly established its role as the site of the imperial residences. The building was begun in the early years of Domitian's reign and in the main completed by 92 AD, although some parts, such as the stadium, were finished later. It was used as the emperor's palace until the end of the Empire. The complex is divided into three parts: the *Domus Flavia*, which was used for state functions, the *Domus Augustana* proper, a private wing, and finally the *stadium*, or large garden in the shape of a circus.

The Domus Augustana represents an important moment in Roman architecture. Here, Domitian's architect Rabirius created what was to become the canonic formula for the dynastic residence: a synthesis of structural functionality–with the division into official and private sectors–and extravagant decoration, in which the blend of curved and straight lines in the ground plan and the illusionistic and perspective effects, already present in Nero's Domus Aurea and here reproposed, were made a near science.

*A view of the ruins
of the Domus Augustana.*

Above, the remains of the octagonal fountain in the Domus Flavia.

DOMUS FLAVIA

This construction consisted of three aisles separated by columns and terminating in an apse. At the center of the structure are the remains of the *Aula Regia*, or throne room, in which the emperor held audience. Significant parts of another room, the **lararium**, or the emperor's private chapel, are also still extant.

The Circus Maximus and the remains of the Domus Augustana.

Museo della Civiltà Romana: detail of a bas-relief
from the first century AD of the races at the Circus Maximus.

The vast arena of the Circus Maximus
as it appears today.

CIRCUS MAXIMUS

Although the Circus Maximus, the first construction of its kind in Rome, was initially built of wood, the sections in masonry gradually increased in number, beginning with the **carceres**, a sort of starting-gate for the horses. The circus consisted of a long track surrounded by a **cavea** with various tiers of seats, broken, on the side adjacent to the Palatine, by the **pulvinar**, a building with a tribune on which were placed the statues of the divinities that presided over the spectacles and from which the emperor watched the contests.

The Circus measured 600 x 200 meters and had a capacity of 320,000 spectators. The most important of the events held there were the chariot races during the first week of September on occasion of the *Ludi Romani*, games which opened with a religious procession in which the highest religious and civil authorities of the city took part. Today, only the lay of the land, much higher than the first arena, betrays the form of the original structure.

1) *Isola Tiberina*   2) *Theater of Marcellus*   3) *Porticus of Octavia*

BOCCA DELLA VERITÀ

At the back of the left side of the portico of the Church of Santa Maria in Cosmedin is a large stone disk representing the frowning face of a river god, commonly known as the Bocca della Verità or "Mouth of Truth." Although it is actually an antique drain cover carved in the form of a mask with an open mouth, the plaque is traditionally held to be an incorruptible judge: those acting in good faith can put their hands in the mouth of the god without fear, but those whose consciences are not quite as spotless and who challenge the judgement of the god run the risk of seeing the mouth snap shut and finding their hands amputated.

The Bocca della Verità under the portico of the Church of Santa Maria in Cosmedin.

The facade of the Church of Santa Maria in Cosmedin.

A detail of the Gothic ciborium and the Cosmatesque pavement.

CHURCH OF SANTA MARIA IN COSMEDIN

When, in the late 19th century, Sardi's beautiful Baroque facade was demolished, the Church of Santa Maria in Cosmedin rediscovered its early medieval aspect. This is in fact the period (6th-7th century) in which the original building was raised in the ruins of the Roman *Annona* and of the 5th-century BC Temple of Ceres. In the **interior** are one of the most beautiful *Cosmatesque pavement* of Rome and an elegant Gothic *ciborium*, a late 14th-century work by Deodatus of Cosma.

The propylaea of the Porticus of Octavia.

The ancient marble market stall from the era in which the Porticus of Octavia was the site of the fish market.

PORTICUS OF OCTAVIA

The complex, built by Augustus between 33 and 23 BC and dedicated to his sister Octavia, was destroyed by the fire of 80 AD and restored by Domitian. A second reconstruction was undertaken by Septimius Severus after another fire in 191 AD. The remains we see today are those of the latter version. The parts of the complex that are still visible and in good condition include the propylaea on the south side, which projected inwards and outwards with two facades consisting of four Corinthian columns topped by pediments, with an inscription on the architrave celebrating the Severian restoration.

A view of a side aisle of the Church of Santa Maria in Cosmedin (above) and the Temple of Vesta.

Above, the Temple of Fortuna Virilis and the Palazzo Orsini, incorporated into the remains of the Theater of Marcellus; right, part of the structures of the theater.

THEATER OF MARCELLUS

The project for the so-called Theater of Marcellus dates to Caesar's time, but the building was finished only in 13 BC by Augustus, who officially dedicated it in the name of his nephew Marcellus, his first designated heir who died prematurely in 23 BC. In the 13th century, the building was occupied by the noble Savelli family; in the 18th century it passed to the Orsinis. The refined Renaissance **palace** that occupies the third floor of the exterior facade of the cavea is the work of the architect Baldassarre Peruzzi. It has been calculated that the cavea (129.80 meters diameter) held between 15,000 and 20,000 spectators, making it the largest theater in Rome as far as audience capacity was concerned.

SYNAGOGUE

The synagogue, or Israelite temple, stands on Via del Portico di Ottavia, along the Tiber. Like other Italian synagogues, it is characterized by a style that can be best classified as "exotic revival," in this case Assyrian-Babylonian. The building terminates in a large aluminum **dome**, a clear indication of its belonging to the early twentieth century; in fact, the synagogue was designed by the architects Armanni and Costa and built in 1904. As the presence of a synagogue would indicate, the area in which it stands was once occupied by the Jewish ghetto.

Rome's synagogue.

IN THE GHETTO

A glimpse down a narrow street, the plaque recalling the rout of 16 October 1943, and the fountain by Landini, named the Fontana delle Tartarughe.

A view of Ponte Cestio and the Ponte Rotto (right).

ISOLA TIBERINA

According to an old written tradition, the small island in the Tiber, now known as the Isola Tiberina, was formed when the grain that had been harvested in the Campus Martius was thrown into the river after the expulsion of the last Etruscan king of this line from Rome. The first important building erected on the island, the Temple of Aesculapius, dates to 291 BC. Although nothing remains today of the original building, it is fairly certain that it stood on the same site as the 17th-century Church of San Bartolomeo. The porticoes of the sanctuary of Aesculapius constituted a true hospital. Thanks to its being isolated from the inhabited areas, the medical tradition of the island continued through the Middle Ages and even in our times, with the *Hospital*

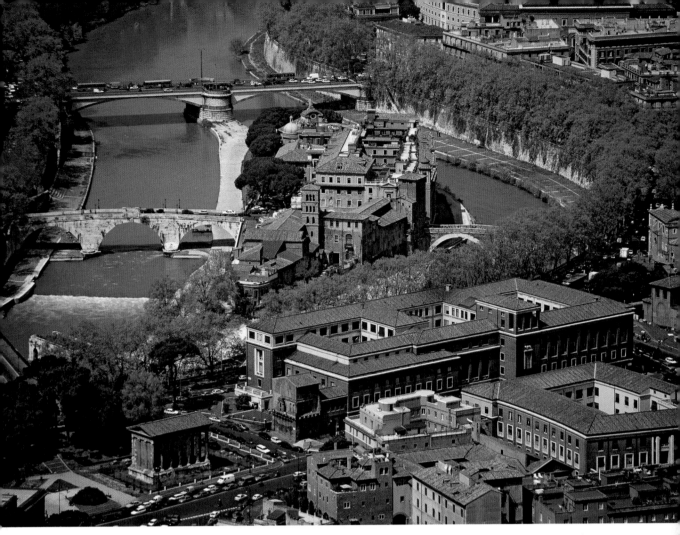

Aerial view of the Isola Tiberina.

The Isola Tiberina and the Ponte Rotto.

of the Fatebenefratelli, adjacent to the small **Church of San Giovanni Calibita**. In antiquity, the island was joined to the city by two bridges. The bridge that still today connects the island to the left bank, near the Theater of Marcellus, is the ancient **Pons Fabricius**. The other bridge, by which the island communicates with Trastevere, is no longer the original one. The ancient **Pons Cestius** was torn down and partially rebuilt between 1888 and 1892. Downstream of the Isola Tiberina are the haunting ruins of the so-called **Ponte Rotto**, a bridge built on the remains of the ancient Roman *Pons Aemilius* of 179 BC. Some would date its origins to the 6th century BC, on the basis of its embankments. The span still standing in midstream dates to the late 16th century, although the pylons on which it rests are still those of the Roman bridge.

Monumental Rome

PIAZZA NAVONA

This square, the most famous of Baroque Rome, covers the site of Domitian's stadium. The name would seem to derive from a popular corruption of the term for the competitive (*in agone*) games that were held here in Roman times. From Domitian onward, the stadium was used almost exclusively for sports events, including the famous regatta held in August, in which the participants wore the colors of the nobles and the civic clergy. Today, the square hosts the Christmas market of the Befana from mid-December to Twelfth Night. But the real attraction is Gianlorenzo Bernini's famous **Fontana dei Quattro Fiumi** (*Fountain of the Four Rivers - 1651*), which won for the artist the admiration and protection of the then-pope Innocent X. The rivers represented in the fountain are the *Danube*, the *Ganges*, the *Nile*, and the *Rio de la Plata*. They are arranged on a steep rocky crag from which a Roman obelisk, taken from the Circus of Maxentius, rises daringly into the air. Aligned with the Fountain of the Four Rivers are the **Fountain of the Moor**, at the south end in front of the **Palazzo Pamphilij**, and the **Fountain of Neptune**, formerly "of the Calderari," at the northern end of the square.

Aerial view of Piazza Navona.

The Church of Sant'Agnese in Agone from the Fontana del Moro or Fountain of the Moor in Piazza Navona.

TO VISIT

Ara Pacis Augustae p. 63
Baths of Diocletian p. 56
Campo de' Fiori p. 51
Castel Sant'Angelo p. 72
Elephant of Piazza della Minerva
 p. 53
Fontana del Tritone p. 62
Fontana di Trevi p. 55
Mausoleum of Augustus p. 64
National Museum of Rome p. 57
Palazzo Barberini and Galleria
 Nazionale d'Arte Antica p. 62
Palazzo and Galleria Spada p. 50
Pantheon p. 52
Piazza del Popolo p. 65
Piazza del Quirinale p. 58
Piazza di Spagna and Trinità
 dei Monti p. 59
Piazza Navona p. 49
Via Veneto p. 62
Villa Borghese p. 67

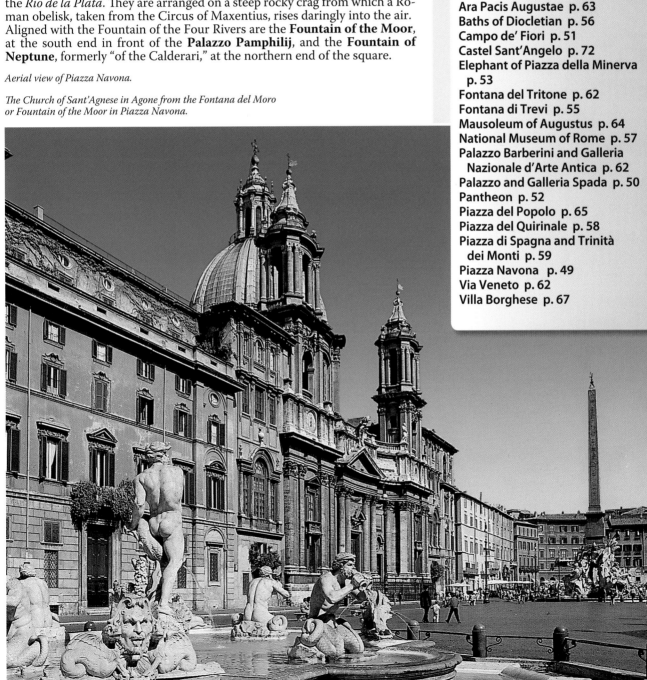

The Fountain of Neptune in Piazza Navona.

Palazzo Spada: the columned "perspective gallery" by Borromini.

PASQUINO

One of the famous 'talking statues' to which the Roman people traditionally posted brief satyric verses ridiculing those in power, called *pasquinades*.

The statue is actually one figure from a Roman sculptural group of *Menelaus Supporting Patrocles*, found in 1501 and installed in its present location by order of Cardinal Oliviero Carafa.

PALAZZO AND GALLERIA SPADA

This palace surprises the visitor, with its architectural affiatus and the imaginative design of the decoration. Borromini made a number of fantastic modifications to the original structure: the most sensational was to create the so-called **Galleria Prospettica**, a corridor 9 meters in length that thanks to peculiar architectural sleights of hand appears instead to be 37 meters long. The *Galleria Spada*, which contains the works of art collected by Cardinal Bernardino Spada, is instead of a completely different nature. Here, works by the most important painters of the 17th century are exhibited in accordance with the tried-and-true criterion of the 17th-century private picture gallery: Titian, Mattia Preti, Baciccia, Guercino, Guido Reni, Annibale Caracci, Rubens, Solimena, and Orazio and Artemisia Gentileschi are only a few of the artists represented here.

Campo de' Fiori

CAMPO DE' FIORI R.VI

The special atmosphere that makes Campo de' Fiori one of Rome's most authentic milieus changes hour by hour, just as its colors and the sounds that invade the fascinating space, bounded by picturesque small buildings and charming shops, make spectrum shifts according to the time of day. In the morning, the brightly-colored **market** fills the square with the voices of the hawkers who sing the praises of their wares: fruit and vegetables, meats and cheeses, clothing and household goods. But in the late morning, as the last of the vendors' stalls are carted away, silence falls as though by magic and the feel of Campo de' Fiori becomes almost intimate, with the only sounds the discreet footfalls of Roman and foreign passers-by. At dusk, especially in summer, the square comes alive again, with visitors attracted by the typical **cafes**, **taverns**, **restaurants**, and **wine-shops** that face on it and the streets off it, while strolling musicians fill the air with their music. In the past, however, the spectacles and pastimes were of quite a different kind: although Campo de' Fiori was the theater of festive events such as horse-races, jousts, and tournaments, it was also the site of executions, including that of the philosopher **Giordano Bruno**, who was accused of heresy and burned at the stake in February of the year 1600, as the 19th-century monument by Ettore Ferrari, at the center of the square, reminds us.

The monument Giordano Bruno, erected in the late 19th century.

Some images suggesting the typical atmosphere of the district. Bottom left, Piazza Farnese.

PANTHEON

Pantheon: the inscription above the pronaos attests to the building's patrimony: "Marcus Agrippa, son of Lucius, consul for the third time, made it."

In the pagan religions, the "pantheon" was the temple dedicated to "all the gods." Over time, the term has come to stand for a mausoleum of illustrious figures. The Panthéon of Paris, for example, in neoclassical style, preserves the remains of such famous men in French history and culture as Jean-Jacques Rousseau and Voltaire, Jean Jaurès, and Jean-Paul Marat. The Pantheon of Rome is one of the most extraordinary of ancient Roman monuments in virtue of its excellent state of preservation, its unequalled grandeur, and its architectural plan, which has been copied time and time again in neoclassical buildings in all parts of the world. Raphael (Raffaello Sanzio) and members of the House of Savoy, Italy's last reigning family, are interred here. Of all the buildings of ancient Rome, the Pantheon is the best preserved, thanks to its having been donated to Pope Boniface IV by the Byzantine emperor Phocas and later transformed into a church with the name of *Santa Maria ad Martyres* (609 AD). The first building was erected in 27 BC by Marcus Vipsanius Agrippa, Augustus' faithful advisor. The temple was conceived for the glorification of the *gens Julia* and was called the Pantheon (*sanctissimum*): all the planetary divinities in addition to Mars and Venus, the protectors of Augustus' family, may have been honored here. Agrippa's building, as excavations carried out in the late 19th century have shown, was rectangular and faced south, not north as now. The temple was damaged in the fire of 80 AD and was restored by Domitian. It was again damaged by fire in Trajan's time, and was completely rebuilt by Hadrian between 118 and 128 AD in the form we still see today. The facade of the large columned **porch** is still composed of eight columns in grey granite. Behind the porch is a massive construction in brick, which joins the porch and the **rotunda**, a gigantic cylinder with a wall that is six meters thick and divided into three superposed sectors marked externally by cornices. The wall lightens as it rises, and moreover is not always solid, being cut through by brick vaulting in various places. The height of the rotunda at the top of the dome is precisely that of its diameter (43.30 meters): the interior space is thus a perfect sphere. The **dome** is a masterpiece of engineering: it is the widest masonry dome ever raised and was cast in a single operation over an enormous wooden framework. The **interior** of the building has six distyle niches at the sides and a semicircular exedra at the back; in between are eight small aediculae with alternating arched and triangular pediments. The dome is decorated with five tiers of hollow coffers that cover it completely except for a smooth band near the *oculus*, the circular opening (9 meters in diameter) that provides the only light to the interior.

The vast interior of the Pantheon with its niches and small chapels.

Another view of the interior of the Pantheon: at the top of the dome is the circular oculus, *the symbol of the solar disk, the building's only source of light.*

The Column of Marcus Aurelius in Piazza della Colonna. The spiral relief commemorates the military victories of Marcus Aurelius.

The tomb of Raphael in the Pantheon.

ELEPHANT OF PIAZZA DELLA MINERVA

Considered one of Bernini's most delightful inventions, the elephant serves as the support for the Egyptian **obelisk** dating to the 6th century BC. Sculpted by Ercole Ferrata in 1667, it is so small in relation to the column that it is popularly known as "Minerva's chick."

The elephant, designed by Bernini, that supports the 6th-century BC Egyptian obelisk in Piazza della Minerva.

FONTANA DI TREVI

This may not be the most beautiful fountain in Rome, but it is without doubt the most famous. Both Pietro da Cortona and above all Bernini, who began the undertaking, had a hand in the project. The death of Pope Urban VIII brought work to a standstill and it was not until about a hundred years later that Clement XII entrusted the work to Nicola Salvi, who finished the fountain between 1732 and 1751.

A tall and sober **Arch of Triumph** (the Palace of Neptune) dominates the scene from on high. A large niche at the center of the arch lends balance and symmetry to the whole ensemble. A smaller niche to the left contains the statue of *Abundance* by F. Valle, above which is a relief

by Andrea Bergondi depicting *Agrippa Approving the Plans for the Aqueduct.* The niche on the right contains the figure of *Salubrity*, also by F. Valle, surmounted by a relief of the *Virgin Showing the Soldiers the Way*, by G. B. Grossi. The central niche seems to impart movement to the commanding figure of *Neptune*, who with a firm hand guides a chariot drawn by two sea horses, known as the *spirited horse* and the *placid horse*, names obviously derived from the way in which the two animals have been represented. As they gallop over the water, the horses are guided in their course by the figures of *Tritons* emerging from the water sculpted by P. Bracci in 1762. The setting all around consists of rocks.

*The jutting mass of the
Fontana di Trevi.*

A general view of the fountain at dusk and the detail of a triton (above).

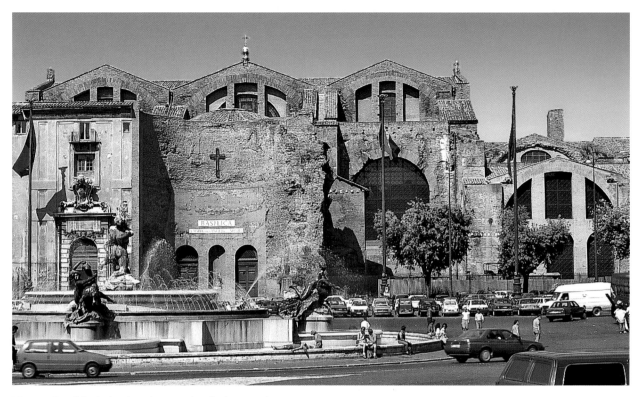

The complex of the Baths of Diocletian and in the foreground the Church of Santa Maria degli Angeli.

BATHS OF DIOCLETIAN

The Baths of Diocletian were in all probability the largest *thermae* ever built in Rome. They went up in a relatively brief period of time, between 298 and 306 AD, under the two Augustan tetrarchs Diocletian and Maximinian, as the dedicatory inscription reminds us. A special branch of the old **Aqua Marcia** aqueduct supplied water for the enormous cistern (91 meters in length), which was demolished once and for all in 1876. Reference to these baths is still to be found in the name "Termini" by which the nearby railroad station is now known. The structures of the original complex of buildings were greatly modified , but the original layout is in part still legible. The main bath building was at the center of a rectangular enclosure with a large semicircular exedra on one of the long sides (corresponding to what is now Piazza della Repubblica), two rotundas at the corners and numerous hemicycles along the perimeter. The plan of the main building is along the lines of the great imperial baths: a large central basilica, the *calidarium-tepidarium-frigidarium* complex on the median axis of the short side, and *palaestrae* and accessory services balancing each other on either side.

The Baths of Diocletian.

Baths of Diocletian: a fresco of a tomb on the Esquiline depicting playing children (1st century).

National Museum of Rome

This museum, housing one of the most important archeological collections in the world, comprises four individual complexes: the **Baths of Diocletian** (which also include the *Octagonal Aula*), **Palazzo Altemps** (where the splendid *Ludovisi collection* is exhibited), **Palazzo Massimo** (with an extraordinary section dedicated to numismatics) and, from 2001, the **Balbi Crypt**.

Palazzo Massimo: detail with an erotic scene from the frescoed wall of the antechamber of cubicle 'D' of the Villa della Farnesina.

Palazzo Altemps: the Birth of Venus *on the* Ludovisi Throne *(5th century BC).*

Baths of Diocletian: the group of Mars and Venus.

Palazzo Massimo: detail of a marble sarcophagus with the Healing of the Blind Man *(4th century).*

Palazzo del Quirinale preceded by the obelisk flanked by two massive Dioscuri from the Roman era.

PIAZZA DEL QUIRINALE

This large square, which in a sense represents the "noble" center of Rome, is overlooked by some of the most interesting buildings of Renaissance, Baroque and rococo Rome (such as the Palazzo del Quirinale, the Palazzo della Consulta, the Church of Sant' Andrea al Quirinale); the fourth, open side is delimited by a theatrical balustrade graced by Roman statues.

Palazzo del Quirinale

Among the architects who worked on the Palazzo del Quirinale were Martino Longhi, Domenico Fontana, Carlo Maderno, Gianlorenzo Bernini, and Ferdinando Fuga, who was also the architect for the Palazzo della Consulta between 1732 and 1734. The Quirinale was the seat of the papacy from Clement XII to 1870, the year in which the complex was chosen as the palace of the kings of united Italy; since 1947 it has been the official residence of the president of the Italian republic.

The curve facade of San Carlo alle Quattro Fontane by Borromini.

Church of San Carlo alle Quattro Fontane

Purely Baroque in its layout, this stunning work by Borromini dates to the middle of the 17th century. The almost "undulating" facade, extremely innovative for the period, catches the light in an inspired play of chiaroscuro.

PIAZZA DI SPAGNA AND TRINITÀ DEI MONTI

One of the most characteristic of Roman squares, Piazza di Spagna runs for 270 meters and is divided into two triangular areas. The square takes its name from the **Palazzo di Spagna**, seat since the 17th century of the Spanish ambassador to the Holy See. It is famous for its magnificent buildings, elegant shops, and for the illustrious personages who sojourned here in the past: from the enigmatic Cagliostro, who held his masonic meetings tinged with magic in an inn, to Casanova, who mentioned the square in his famous *Memoirs*, to Keats, who lived and died at No. 26, now a small **museum** dedicated to the great poet. Other notable buildings, such as the **Palazzo di Propaganda Fide** with the conjoined **Church of the Re Magi**, and the aforementioned complex of the Palazzo di Spagna, also overlook the square.

At the center of the square is the **Fontana della Barcaccia**, set against the theatrical backdrop of the famous **Scalinata di Trinità dei Monti** (or the *Spanish Steps*), which leads to the equally famous **Piazza di Trinità dei Monti** with the **Sallustian obelisk**, formerly in the Horti Sallustiani, at its center. This square is dominated by the bulk of the **Church of Trinità dei Monti**.

Left, a detail of the Sallustian obelisk.

The Church of Trinità dei Monti with the celebrated flight of steps and the Fontana della Barcaccia at dusk.

FONTANA DELLA BARCACCIA

Perhaps the most congenial work by Pietro Bernini, father of the more famous Gianlorenzo, this fountain (1627-1629) stands at the center of the Piazza di Spagna and acts as a sort of fulcrum for the many buildings all around. It is a lively and brilliantly-conceived representation of a sinking boat leaking water at the stern and prow. The idea seems to have come from Pope Urban VIII, who was struck by the sight of a boat that had sunk when the Tiber flooded.

Church of Trinità dei Monti: the single broad nave is home to precious works of art.

SPANISH STEPS OR SCALINATA DI TRINITÀ DEI MONTI

The theatrical effect of these famous steps and their powerful evocative quality is part of the history of the image of the city. Built entirely in travertine by Francesco De Sanctis between 1723 and 1726, the Scalinata consists of twelve flights which widen and narrow in compact but varied stages in no way bound by rigid schemes, in line with rococo architectural concepts. The steps begin in Piazza di Spagna and rise to Piazza di Trinità dei Monti.

CHURCH OF TRINITÀ DEI MONTI

One of the most impressive of the Franciscan churches in the city, Trinità dei Monti was begun in 1503 by Louis XII, but has been remodeled over the course of time. The sober facade, by Carlo Maderno, is preceded by a staircase designed by Domenico Fontana (1587).

A side ramp of the Trinità dei Monti stairs (Spanish Steps).

The Fontana del Tritone at the center of Piazza Barberini.

FONTANA DEL TRITONE

Still another fascinating fountain by Gianlorenzo Bernini is that which has stood at the center of Piazza Barberini since 1643, famous for the apparent lack of any kind of architectural support for the statue of the *Triton* from which it takes its name. He is in fact supported by a scallop shell that in turn rests on the arched tails of four dolphins; the spray of water that animates the whole ensemble is naturalistically blown upwards by the Triton through a conch.

PALAZZO BARBERINI AND THE GALLERIA NAZIONALE D'ARTE ANTICA

The rooms of the palace are the showcase for the Roman statues and antiquities amassed by the Barberini family over the years and to a fine picture collection that is today the nucleus of the Galleria Nazionale d'Arte Antica founded in 1895. The absolute masterpiece of this collection, which includes, among many others, works by Filippo Lippi, Perugino, Bronzino, Tintoretto, Guido Reni, Guercino and many foreign masters, is Raphael's *La Fornarina*, in which criticism traditionally sees the portrait of the woman the artist "loved until his death." Particular interest also invests the *Judith and Holophernes* by Caravaggio and the *Narcissus* for many years attributed to the Baroque painter but now believed by criticism to have been painted by one of his pupils.

Besides the picture gallery, the palace also sported a library and, above all, many architectural features conceived to support its role as a reception facility. Among these were the famous theater designed by Pietro da Cortona, a spheristerion (no longer existing), and the immense space in front of the building in which fêtes and carrousels were held.

The facade of Palazzo Barberini.

Galleria Nazionale d'Arte Antica: Filippo Lippi, the Annunciation.

The Ara Pacis (bottom) and the elegant protective structure designed by architect Richard Meier.

A detail of the freize of the Procession *on the Ara Pacis.*

ARA PACIS AUGUSTAE

The altar was begun on 4 July in 13 BC, near the Via Flaminia on property belonging to Agrippa. The *dedicatio* (that is, the inauguration ceremony upon completion of the work) was held on 30 January in 9 BC. The discovery of the Ara Pacis dates to 1568; in 1870, von Duhn identified these marble fragments for the first time as remains of the famous monument. Systematic excavations begun in 1903 brought to light the supporting structures of the altar; the excavations were finally terminated, in 1937-1938, on occasion of the Augustan bimillenial celebrations, and the altar was reconstructed in a pavilion built for this purpose next to the Mausoleum of Augustus, near the Tiber. The monument is composed of a rectangular marble enclosure on a podium. It was originally accessed via a staircase, with two large doors that opened on the long. The altar itself, set on a three-stepped podium, is inside the enclosure; on the west, five other steps permitted the priest to reach the top of the altar on which the sacrificial rites took place. The entire enclosure is covered with rich sculptural decoration both inside and out.

THE NEW DISPLAY OF THE ARA PACIS AUGUSTAE

Travertine, plaster, glass and steel are the materials that enclose the Ara Pacis in a protective shell creating a museum and defending it against damage from smog. Natural light that streams in from the skylights combines with and enhances the artificial light to reveal the beautiful translucence and shadings of the marble altar.

An aereal view of the Ara Pacis
and the Mausoleum of Augustus.

A view of the Mausoleum of Augustus.

MAUSOLEUM OF AUGUSTUS

The dynastic tomb of the first emperor of Rome is a circular structure consisting of a series of concentric walls in tufa connected by walls radiating out from the center. The first accessible chamber lies at the end of the long entrance corridor (*dromos*) which cuts through the structures described above. Two entrances in this wall lead to the annular corridor which rings the circular cella. The tomb of Augustus was here, in correspondence to the bronze statue of the emperor that stood at the top of the pier.

PIAZZA DEL POPOLO

Piazza del Popolo, one of the most characteristic areas of Neoclassical Rome, is the child of Giuseppe Valadier's creative genius in the field of town planning and architecture. The original design dates to 1793. Distinctive features of the square are the low exedrae defining its sides, topped by statues of the *Four Seasons*, and the two centrally-placed fountains, *Neptune and the Tritons and Rome between the Tiber and the Aniene Rivers*, that set off the obelisk. All the sculpture dates to the first half of the 19th century and is the work of Gnaccarini, Laboureur, Stocchi, Baini, and Ceccarini.

GOETHE MUSEUM

The Goethe Museum, in Via del Corso 17, occupies the rooms where the author of *Italian Journey* lived during his stay in Rome from 1786 to 1788. The museum preserves portraits of J. Wolfgang von Goethe (one by Andy Warhol!), drawings by J. H. W. Tischbein, a close friend of the author, works by Goethe, and many other books on the history of cultural relations between Germany and Italy.

A view, from the Pincian Hill, of Piazza del Popolo and the Flaminian obelisk.

Monumental Rome

Above, the Casino Borghese, residence of Cardinal Scipione.

Detail of the fountain known as the 'Fontana degli Ippocampi' by Cristoforo Unterberger (1791).

Facing page, the Giardino del Lago with the Temple of Aesculapius (above) and the Garden of Venus.

The Fountain of Venus in the garden of the same name.

VILLA BORGHESE

The villa and its park were designed for Cardinal Scipione Caffarelli Borghese in the early 1600s; although the villa was completely remodeled at the end of the following century. The park is the largest in the city, all of six kilometers around its perimeter, and it is also the loveliest and the most fascinating. In the midst of luxuriant plant life and a wealth of decorative elements lies a small artificial lake surrounded by an elegant garden known as the **Giardino del Lago**. An Ionic **temple** dedicated to Aesculapius, built in the late 18th century, rises on the island at the center. A little further on are evocative avenues leading to **Piazza di Siena**, designed as an amphitheater. Every year horse-lovers gather here to watch one the most famous equestrian events in the world.

Museum and Gallery

The green slope of the Pincio overlooking Via Flaminia was chosen in 1608 by Cardinal Scipione Borghese as the site for a suburban villa immersed in an enormous park. The recently-restored *palazzina*, also called the **Casino Borghese**, hosts the **Museo** and the **Galleria Borghese**, two of the most celebrated art collections in the world. Both got their start with Cardinal Scipione, who brought together not only many paintings but also antiquities of different origin and entrusted their restoration to the greatest artists of the time.

First and foremost among these masters was Gianlorenzo Bernini (1598-1680), who also created for his rich benefactor certain among the absolute masterpieces of Baroque statuary: the *David*, sculpted in 1623-1624, whose countenance is the self-portrait of the artist, and *Apollo and Daphne*, a marble group sculpted during the same period but of mythological inspiration, as was the *Rape of Proserpine*, an early but brilliant work. In 1807, Prince Camillo Borghese sold the collection to his cousin, Napoleon Bonaparte, who carried off many pieces to the Louvre where they still form the main nucleus of the classical antiquities section. Two years earlier, Camillo's wife Pauline had been portrayed by Canova in the pose of *Venus*, a work that still today is one of the major attractions of the museum.

Above, Museo Borghese:
Gianlorenzo Bernini,
The Rape of Proserpine *(1622).*

Museo Borghese: Antonio Canova,
Paolina Borghese Bonaparte
as Venus Victrix *(1805).*

Museo Borghese:
Gianlorenzo Bernini,
Apollo and Daphne
(1604).

Museo Borghese: Gianlorenzo Bernini,
Bust of Scipione Borghese.

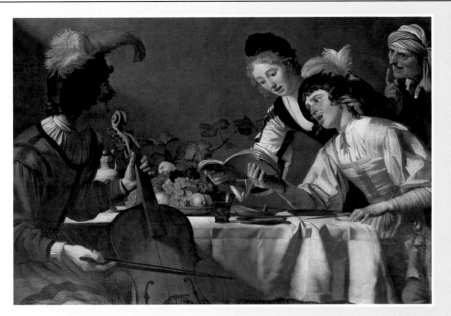

Galleria Borghese: Gerrit von Honthorst, The Concert (1620).

RENAISSANCE PAINTING

Like the collection of statues and antiquities, the collection of paintings that today graces the **Galleria Borghese** was also begun by Cardinal Scipione, who assembled a great number of masterpieces by the most illustrious exponents of 16th- and 17th-century painting. Caravaggio is represented here with some of his

Galleria Borghese: Titian (Tiziano Vecellio), Sacred and Profane Love (1514).

Galleria Borghese: Giorgione, (attrib.), Singer with Flute.

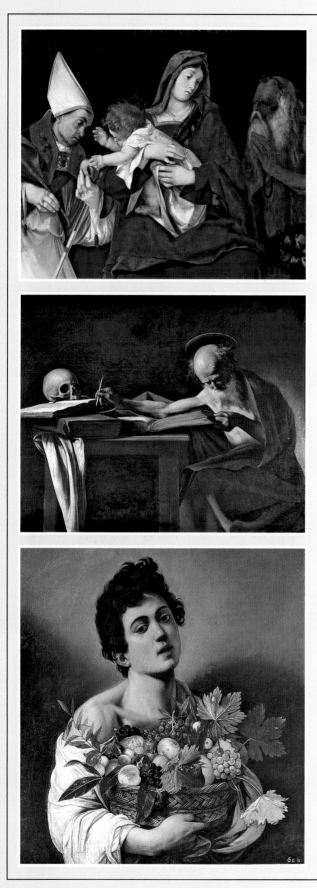

most interesting and most evocative works: the *Boy with a Fruit Basket*, one of the master's first Roman works, the *Little Bacchus*, the *Madonna dei Palafrenieri*, *Saint Jerome*, and the *David with the head of Goliath*, one of his last works, in which the slain giant wears his countenance. Alongside the works by the great Baroque artist from Lombardy, Cardinal Scipione collected paintings of enormous value by Raphael (the *Entombment of Christ*, perhaps better known as the *Borghese Deposition*), Titian (*Sacred and Profane Love*), and painters of the Ferrarese school (*Apollo* by Dosso Dossi). Later acquisitions (including the addition of the collection of Olimpia Aldobrandini, wife of Paolo Borghese) brought to the gallery such masterpieces as the *Virgin and Child with Young Saint John and Angels* by Botticelli, Correggio's *Danaë*, the *Portrait of a Man* by Antonello da Messina and works by many other Italian and foreign masters (Domenichino, Lorenzo Lotto, Parmigianino, Veronese, Rubens, and Cranach).

Above, Galleria Borghese: Lorenzo Lotto, Holy Conversation *(1508).*

Galleria Borghese: Caravaggio, left, Saint Jerome *(1605-1606), bottom left,* Boy with a Fruit Basket *(1594 circa) and, bottom,* Sick Little Bacchus *(1592-1595).*

Villa Giulia and the Etruscan Museum

O ne of the most fanciful realizations of architectural Mannerism is Villa Giulia, built for Pope Julius III in the area called the Vigna Vecchia against the walls of the city. Villa Giulia was chosen in 1889 to house the rich collection of **Etruscan antiquities** and relics of the Italic civilizations that flourished between the Iron Age and the beginning of Roman hegemony in the territory between the lower Tiber valley and Tuscany.

Museo Etrusco di Villa Giulia: the head of Leucothea, "white goddess" of the sea (terracotta, 4th century BC).

Museo Etrusco di Villa Giulia: head of Silenus, fictile antefix from Pyrgi.

Museo Etrusco di Villa Giulia: the Husband and Wife Sarcophagus (6th cent. BC).

Museo Etrusco di Villa Giulia: an Attic amphora depicting Achilles and Ajax throwing dice.

Aranciera di Villa Borghese

T he Aranciera di Villa Borghese (Orangery), which predates Cardinal Scipione Borghese's villa, has been modified and enlarged many times over the course of its centuries of history. Today, its first floor hosts the **Museo Carlo Bilotti**, named for the donor of the collection displayed here, while the ground floor is a splendid venue for temporary exhibits.

The Aranciera.

Aranciera di Villa Borghese, Museo Carlo Bilotti: Giorgio De Chirico: Hector and Andromache (bronze, h. 230 cm).

*Castel Sant'Angelo from the bridge of the same name,
to which Gianlorenzo Bernini added statues of angels.*

CASTEL SANT'ANGELO

*The bronze statue of the
Archangel Michael atop
the fortress.*

Castel Sant'Angelo was originally the *mausoleum of the emperor Hadrian,* designed and ordered built by Hadrian himself in 130 AD as his final resting place and that of all the members of the Antonine dynasty. The overall aspect of the construction was that of an immense tumulus grave, of Etruscan derivation and built on the model of the Mausoleum of Augustus. The sepulchral chamber at the center of the mausoleum, which housed the cinerary urns of the emperor and his family members and later those of all his successors up to Caracalla, was reached through a helicoidal gallery. Even under Aurelian, in fact, the *Hadrian's Mausoleum,* while still preserving its role as a place of burial, had become part of the defensive system created to defend Ponte Helios, today's **Ponte Sant'Angelo**, which performed the func-

tion of access ramp to the mausoleum. In about 520, Theodoric transformed the building into a State prison, a role it was destined to play until 1901 (among others, Cellini and Cagliostro were held prisoners here). He also made it a fortress, to which use it was consecrated at the time of the Gothic War that bloodied Rome for a lengthy period. Some decades after the end of the conflict, in 590, the plague descended to afflict the city. Saint Gregory the Great was pope at the time; one day, as he crossed the bridge in front of the mausoleum, he saw at the summit of the conical roof an angel sheathing a flaming sword, which he took as a sign that the epidemic would soon cease. From that moment on the fortress took the name of Castel Sant'Angelo, but only later, in 1544, was the episode commemorated with the installation of a marble statue of the *Archangel Michael* by Raffaello da Montelupo in the place the apparition had been seen. The original angel was replaced in 1752 by the bronze copy by Verschaffelt. During the Middle Ages, the fortress became especially important for defense of the Vatican, above all from the 9th century, when Pope Leo IV made it an integral part of that system of walls that delimited the area known as the "Leonine City" and that connected it to many other buildings, including the nearby Vatican Palace. In the 13th century, under Pope Nicholas III, an overhead corridor

An aerial view of the fortress and the bridge.

View of the interior of Castel Sant'Angelo.

was added along this stretch of the walls. Known as the _Passetto_ or the _Borgo Corridor_, it was restructured and perfected in the following centuries to permit the popes to reach Castel Sant'Angelo quickly in case of danger; the corridor was also used for secretly conducting prelates or nobles suspected of crimes into the prisons in the fortress. As part of the actions targeting improvement of the defenses of the Leonine City carried out in the late 15th century, the first pope of the modern age, Alexander VI, had Giuliano da Sangallo reinforce the castle with construction of a _four-sided surrounding with four octagonal corner towers_ named for the four evangelists, a series of new bastions, and a wide moat. A few years later, under Julius II, the _marble loggia_ overlooking the Tiber was added; Paul III, fearing a Turkish invasion of the coasts of Latium, commissioned Antonio Sangallo the Younger to completely restore the defensive installations and to enlarge the _papal apartments_ in the castle. The rooms were decorated by Perin del Vaga and his studio in the mid-sixteenth century with cycles of frescoes inspired by the history of the Church, as in the _Sala Paolina_ (or Sala del Consiglio), and by figures from classical mythology, as in the rooms known as the _Camera del Perseo_ and the _Camera di Amore and Psyche_. But for the most part, Castel Sant'Angelo still conserves the character of a fortress built for defense, with its armed bastions complete with batteries of cannon, the Armory of Clement X built by Bernini and later transformed into the Chapel of the Condannati, the so-called "Oliare," large rooms and silos used to store foodstuffs for use in case of siege, and the parapet walk, which still today offers the visitor a full view of the Vatican and indeed a goodly portion of the city of Rome.

Monumental Rome   73

The Vatican

VATICAN CITY

Vatican City lies between Monte Mario to the north and the Janiculum to the south. In Roman times, the area now covered by the small Vatican State was called the *Ager Vaticanus* and was occupied by a circus and by Nero's gardens. Since 1929, the year in which the Lateran Treaty was stipulated between the Holy See and the Italian State, Vatican City has been an independent sovereign state. In addition to being the head of the Apostolic Roman Catholic Church, the Pope has full legislative, executive and judiciary powers. Vatican City is completely independent of the Italian State, even though the two maintain extremely friendly relations. The Vatican prints its own stamps and has its own railroad station and a well-known Italian-language newspaper, the *Osservatore Romano*, which is distributed throughout Italy. The city also has its own security service (once called the "pontifical carabinieri") and a real police force: the famous "Swiss Guards" who since the early 16th century have protected the person of the pope.

TO VISIT

Saint Peter's Basilica p. 78
Saint Peter's Square p. 78
Sistine Chapel p. 92
Vatican Palaces p. 86

Nocturnal view of Saint Peter's Basilica.

Aerial view of Saint Peter's Square and Bernini's colonnade.

THE SWISS GUARD

When the Pontifical Swiss Guard was instituted, in 1506, the Swiss Confederation had already been loaning its troops, who were widely known as excellent mercenary soldiers, to European courts in exchange for foodstuffs and trade privileges. The Vatican guard unit was created to counter the threat of aggression against the Papal State from outside forces. Contrary to all expectations, during an extremely violent engagement at the time of the Sack of Rome (1527) the Swiss Guard was routed and massacred by the united Spanish and Lansquenet (German mercenary) forces, who had penetrated into the Vatican to the Raphael Rooms, which they sacked. New guards are sworn in every year on May 6, the anniversary of this battle. Today, the duties of the Guard are to stand guard in certain areas of the Vatican Palaces and to defend the Pope during liturgical ceremonies and as he moves within the Vatican and travels outside its walls. Candidates applying to serve in the Guard must be single male Swiss citizens of the Roman Catholic faith, between 19 and 30 years of age, and must meet the height requirement of 1.74 meters. The minimum term of service is two years. It is commonly accepted that the sumptuous, Renaissance-looking dress uniform of the Guard, with its ample pleats, was designed by Michelangelo.

The facade of Saint Peter's Basilica and Michelangelo's soaring dome (right).

SAINT PETER'S SQUARE

The square was built over a part of the ancient Vatican Circus (or Nero's Circus, though actually built by Caligula), of which there remains the so-called **Vatican Obelisk**, transported here in 37 AD from Alexandria, where it decorated Caesar's Forum. Called in medieval times the *aguglia*, it stood at length beside the basilica, until 1586, when Sixtus V ordered Carlo Maderno to move it to its present site. In 1613, Paul V bid the same Maderno build a fountain to its right; half a century later, a "twin" fountain by Carlo Fontana, placed symmetrically with respect to the first, was added. Again under Sixtus V, the original bronze globe that topped the obelisk (today in the Capitoline Museums) and that was believed to contain the ashes of Caesar was replaced with that Pope's family emblem, the mountains and the star, topped by a crucifix containing a fragment of the Holy Cross of Christ's Crucifixion. In the mid-17th century, when the monumental work of rebuilding Saint Peter's Basilica was well-delineated, attention naturally shifted to the square before it. The fervent activity then being concluded provided the impetus for the sumptuous design of the square, which was built by Gianlorenzo Bernini between 1656 and 1667.

SAINT PETER'S BASILICA

In the classical period, Nero's Circus stood on what is now the site of Saint Peter's, between the Tiber, the Janiculum, and the Vatican hill. Saint Peter, the Prince of the Apostles, was martyred and then buried here in 64 AD. Pope Anacletus had a small *ad corpus* basilica, or a simple shrine, built here. In 324, the emperor Constantine replaced the presumably modest shrine with a true basilica. The original Saint Peter's was completed in 349 by Constantius, son of Constantine, and over the centuries was embellished and renovated by donations and the restoration work carried out by the Popes and munificent princes. It was in Constantine's basilica that Charlemagne received the crown from the hands of Leo III

The Vatican

A view of the monumental interior of Saint Peter's Basilica.

The statue of Saint Peter attributed to Arnolfo di Cambio.

in 800; Lothair, Louis II, and Frederick III were also crowned emperors after him. Even so, a thousand years after its foundation, Saint Peter's was falling into ruin. In 1452, Pope Nicholas V, on the advice of Leon Battista Alberti, appointed Bernardo Rossellino to renovate and enlarge the Basilica to the latter's plan. Work was not resumed until 1506, under Pope Julius II della Rovere, and this time the planned intervention was radical. Most of the original church was dismantled by Bramante (who earned himself the title of *maestro ruinante*), who intended building a "modern" building in the Classical style, from the ground up, on a Greek-cross plan inspired by the Pantheon. Various architects and works supervisors–Fra' Giocondo, Raphael, Giuliano da Sangallo, Baldassarre Peruzzi, and Antonio da Sangallo the Younger–succeeded each other until about the middle of the century until finally, in 1547, Michelangelo was appointed by Paul III. Needless to say, Michelangelo followed his own interpretation of Bramante's plan: he modified and simplified it in part, and designed a soaring **dome** (originally hemispherical) to crown the renovated

basilica. Michelangelo was succeeded by Vignola, Pirro Ligorio, Giacomo Della Porta, and Domenico Fontana, all of whom interpreted Michelangelo's ideas quite faithfully. Then, under Paul V, it was decided to expand the basilica and return to the Latin cruciform plan. With this in mind, the architect Carlo Maderno added three chapels to each side of the building and brought the nave as far as the present **facade**, the building of which was entrusted to him when he won an important competition. Work on the facade was begun in November of 1607 and terminated in 1614. After the death of Carlo Maderno in 1629, the next director of works was Gianlorenzo Bernini, who left his unmistakable mark on the building: the prevalently Baroque character it now displays was his doing. It is sufficient to mention the erection of the justly-famous bronze **Baldacchino** (begun in 1624 and inaugurated on Saint Peter's Day in 1633) over the Papal Altar, the decoration of the piers of the dome with four large statues, and, of course, the placing of the *Throne of Saint Peter* at the back of the apse. This is one of Bernini's most sumptuous inventions, a truly marvelous machine

built around the old wooden chair which a pious tradition says was used by the apostle Peter. The layout of Saint Peter's Square, once more by Bernini, also dates to the papacy of Alexander VII (who financed the works for the throne). It was instead under Clement X that the architect designed and built the small round temple which is the tabernacle of the Chapel of the Holy Sacrament. Any number of chapels, all splendid in one way or the other, line the perimeter of Saint Peter's Basilica: to begin with, the **Chapel of the Pietà**, named after Michelangelo's famous marble sculpture of the *Pietà* made between 1499 and 1500, when the artist was still a young man, for Cardinal Jean de Bilhères. After the **Chapel of Saint Sebastian** (which contains Francesco Messina's *monument to Pope Pius XII*) comes the better-known **Chapel of the Holy Sacrament**, with the tabernacle by Bernini and the elaborate bronze railings designed by Borromini; next is the **Gregorian Chapel**, a late 16th-century work completed by Giacomo Della Porta and heavily decorated with mosaics and precious marbles, the **Colonna Chapel**, the sumptuous

Above, Bernini's "Gloria" with the Cathedra Petri *or Throne of Saint Peter at its center.*

Left, Bernini's magnificent monument to Pope Alexander VII.

Bottom, a view of the interior of Michelangelo's dome.

A religious ceremony in Saint Peter's Basilica. Bernini's celebrated Baldachin towers above the Papal Altar.

The Vatican

The tomb of Saint Peter and, on the left, that of Pope John Paul II.

the *bronze tomb* created by Antonio Pollaiolo *for Pope Innocent VIII*, and the Neoclassical *Stuart Monument* by Canova. The great sacristy rises before the left transept. As large as a church, and in fact originally conceived as an independent building, the sacristy consists of the **Sacrestia Comune** on an octagonal central plan, the so-called **Sacristy of the Canons**, and the **Chapter Hall**. It was all designed by the Roman architect Carlo Marchionni at the behest of Pius VI, who laid the first stone in 1776. Annexed to the basilica is the **Museo della Fabbrica di San Pietro**, or Historical Artistic Museum, which includes the *Treasury of Saint Peter's*. It was designed by Giovan Battista Giovenale and contains what remains of the enormous artistic patrimony of the church which was repeatedly broken up and carried off during the Saracen raids, the Sack of Rome in 1527, and the Napoleonic confiscations.

Chapel of the Choir, the **Chapel of the Presentation**, with the recent *monument to Pope John XXIII* by Emilio Greco. Saint Peter's Basilica in fact contains a whole collection of famous monuments, from Michelangelo's *Pietà* to the venerated 13th-century *effigy of Saint Peter* shown in the act of blessing, to Bernini's *funeral monument to Pope Urban VIII*, the analogous *funeral monument to Pope Paul III*, by Guglielmo Della Porta,

Vatican Grottoes

The grottoes, situated under the nave of Saint Peter's Basilica, contain the tombs of many Popes, as well as early Christian sarcophagi, architectural fragments and various monuments from the Basilica. The area embraces two sections, known as the *New Grottoes* and the *Old Grottoes*.

MICHELANGELO IN ROME

Michelangelo's work in Rome is an essential aspect of the landscape of the papal capital, which the artist interpreted in all its grandeur as no other before or since. From the plans for Piazza del Campidoglio and Porta Pia, and the final plan for Saint Peter's Basilica—from Michelangelo architect—to the important sculptural group of the *Pietà* (1499-1500), a fixture and attraction of the basilica, to the Sistine Chapel frescoes, everything he did in Rome speaks of an artist capable of conceiving and carrying out large-scale projects in harmony with the wishes of his patron—in this case the papacy—who saw him as the true heir of classical art: "Gloria del secolo nostro" as he was defined by Pope Paul III. Michelangelo (Caprese M. 1475 - Rome 1564) was invited to Rome in 1508 by Pope Julius II della Rovere to fresco the vault of the Sistine Chapel, which until his time had been decorated with gold stars on a blue field. Creation of what is considered Michelangelo's greatest masterpiece and the city's best-known work of art cost the artist years of backbreaking work alone on special scaffolding, and conflicts with the papal court as he attempted to wrest maximum freedom of artistic expression from his patrons. 1515 is the date of the gigantic statue of *Moses* in the Basilica of San Pietro in Vincoli, a complement to the Mausoleum of Julius II della Rovere commissioned by the pope before his death.

Saint Peter's Basilica: Michelangelo, the Pietà.

Michelangelo returned to Rome in 1534, during the pontificate of Clement VI de' Medici, to fresco the end wall of the Sistine Chapel with the famous *Last Judgment*. The artist lived in the Eternal City until his death, supported by a life stipend granted by Pope Paul III Farnese.

A bird's-eye view of the Vatican Museums.

VATICAN PALACES

One of the most sumptuous monumental complexes in the world is certainly that of the Vatican Palaces, built from the 14th century, which over the centuries were worked on by some of the most important Italian artists, like Michelangelo, Bramante, Raphael and Bernini. Michelangelo produced the fabulous frescoes in the **Sistine Chapel** (commissioned by Sixtus IV and built between 1473 and 1480) and those of the **Pauline Chapel** and **Sala Regia**. Bramante was responsible for the creation of the **Cortile del Belvedere** and the elevation of the **loggias of the Cortile di San Damaso**, later frescoed by Raphael, like the splendid **Stanze**. Lastly, Bernini created the **Scala Regia** and the **Sale Paoline** of the library and archive. Today these buildings also house the Vatican Museums.

Vatican Museums

From the very first, the complex that is today called the Vatican Palaces and that is the result of a long process of construction and transformation has hosted splendid collections of art assembled by the various Popes, including the celebrated **Pinacoteca Vaticana**. The buildings gradually became museums to all effects; the first step in this direction was taken in the latter half of the 18th century by Clement XIV, who transformed the Palazzetto del Belvedere into the museum that following the reorganization ordered by Clement's successor Pius VI took the name of **Museo Pio-Clementino**. In the first half of the following century, that passion for archaeology and antiquity that was a hallmark of Neoclassical taste induced two Popes, Pius VII and Gregory XVI, to create one of the cardinal institutions of the Vatican Museum complex: the former was responsible for the foundation of the **Museo Chiaramonti**, to the decoration of which even Canova contributed and for which the so-called Braccio Nuovo was expressly built in 1816; the latter, instead, organized the **Museo Gregoriano Etrusco** and the **Museo Gregoriano Egizio** in seventeen rooms. Later on in the 19th century, Pope Leo XIII opened to the public many rooms which theretofore had been reserved for the Pope and the

highest members of the ecclesiastical hierarchy. The first such revelation was the Borgia Apartments, the rooms of which later became the seat of the **Collection of Modern Religious Art** inaugurated by Pope Paul VI in 1973. The creation of new museums went on all through the 20th century: John XXIII had both the **Museo Missionario-Etnologico**, instituted in 1926 to house the material exhibited at the **Missionary Exhibit of the 1925 Jubilee**, and the **Museo Pio Cristiano,** founded in 1854 by Pius IX to organize the paintings, inscriptions, reliefs and sculptures from the catacombs and the ancient Roman basilicas.

A detail of the portal by Cecco Bonanotte.

The new architecture of the entrance to the Vatican Museums.

NEW ENTRANCE TO THE VATICAN MUSEUMS

The new entrance to the Vatican Museums, that was opened in 2000 has provided a rational solution for coping with the ever-increasing number of people who visit the museum complex. The construction work involved the creation of a new, four-storey building between the 18th century Museo Pio-Clementino and the old 16th century walls. A broad, **helicoidal ramp** that is 165 meters long leads visitors to the exhibition rooms via the Cortile delle Corazze that was covered by a glass and metal roof.

Two images of the gracious spiral ramp leading to the exhibition rooms of the Vatican Museums.

Raphael Rooms

The master began frescoing what are now known as the Stanze di Raffaello (Raphael Rooms) in 1509. The work, which continued into the following years under Leo X, revolves around themes that celebrate the power of Faith and the Church. The first room to be frescoed was the **Stanza della Segnatura**, or **Signature Room**, called thus because it was here that the Pope signed official documents; Raphael's sure touch gleams from all the frescoes in this magnificent room, from the *Dispute of the Blessed Sacraments*, depicting the glorification of the Eucharist, to the *School of Athens*, where within a grandiose architectural frame the wise men and the philosophers of ancient times are set side by side with the seigneurs and the artists of the Renaissance cultural scene, all gathered around the figures of Plato and Aristotle, and to the *Parnassus*, an allegorical celebration of the arts impersonated by the mythological figures of the Muses and the pagan gods. In the alternating medallions and panels of the ceiling, almost as though to offer a symbolic compendium of the frescoes on the walls below, Raphael painted a number of allegorical representations of the *Sciences* and the *Arts* (*Theology, Justice, Philosophy, Poetry, Astronomy*) together with emblematic episodes referred to them (*Adam and Eve*, the *Judgement of Solomon, Apollo and Marsyas*). Between 1512 and 1514, Raphael worked on the decoration of the **Room of Heliodorus**, where he frescoed historical episodes in accordance with an iconographic program dictated by Julius II: *Leo I Halting Attila*, alluding to the battle of Ravenna in 1512 at which the future Leo X defeated the French; the *Miracle at Bolsena*, illustrating the institution of the *Corpus Domini* by Urban IV and also calling to mind the vow made by Julius II before the siege of Bologna; the biblical episode of the *Expulsion of Heliodorus from the Temple*, which refers to the Pope's struggle against the enemies of the Church; and finally the *Liberation of Saint Peter*, alluding to the liberation of Leo X, who was imprisoned following the battle of Ravenna. The next two years were dedicated to the **Room of the Fire in the Borgo**, which takes its name from the principal fresco, *The Borgo Fire* of 847 AD, inspired by the figure of Leo IV who quenched the fire by making the sign of the Cross. This fresco and the other three in the room (the *Battle of Ostia*, the *Oath of Leo III*, the *Coronation of Charlemagne*), executed almost entirely by Raphael's pupils under the strict guidance of the master, make specific reference to the illustrious predecessors of Leo X, during whose pontificate the room was decorated, who bore his same name. The **Sala dei Palafrenieri** also contained wall paintings by Raphael, which were destroyed and later replaced by other frescoes ordered by Gregory XIII in the late 1500s. The decoration of the **Hall of Constantine**, instead, is certainly the work of one of Raphael's most important followers, Giulio Romano. Following the death of the master he led a team of artists who illustrated in fresco episodes from the life of Constantine: the *Baptism of Constantine*, the *Battle of the Milvian Bridge*, the *Apparition of the Cross*, and *Constantine's Donation*.

Stanza della Segnatura (Signature Room):
Raphael, The School of Athens.

Stanza della Segnatura (Signature Room): Raphael, Dispute of the Blessed Sacraments.

RAPHAEL'S LOGGIA

One of the most significant corners in the entire Vatican palace complex, the lovely, airy loggia was begun by Bramante but terminated by Raphael in about 1518. Twelve of the 13 bays with pavilion vaults (an inspired architectural solution) are frescoed with scenes from the *Old Testament*, while the last is decorated with stories of the *New Testament*. The frescoes, all exhibiting an extreme freshness and an imaginative use of perspective, are the work of some of Raphael's most illustrious pupils, such as Giulio Romano, Polidoro da Caravaggio, Giovanni da Udine, Perin del Vaga, Pellegrino Aretusi da Modena, and Vincenzo da San Gimignano.

Stanza di Eliodoro (Heliodorus Room): Raphael, Expulsion of Heliodorus from the Temple.

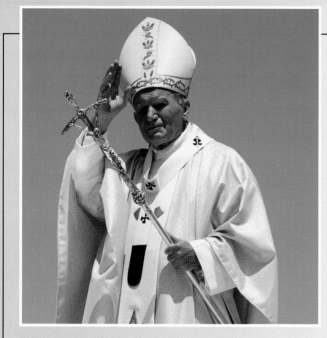

THE FIGURE OF THE POPE

As well as being the head of the Roman Apostolic Catholic Church, the Pope is also bishop of the diocese of Rome and head of the Vatican City State. The word "pope" comes from the Greek *pappas* ("father") and was used from the 3rd century onwards. The pontiff is elected by bishops, meeting in conclave, with a secret vote that requires a two-thirds majority. Four votes a day are held: the emission of a black smoke signal indicates a negative outcome, whereas white smoke signifies the successful election of the new pope, who is hailed with the celebrated *Habemus papam* ("We have a pope"). The Pope lives in an apartment in the Vatican Palaces; other residences are the Lateran Palace and Castel Gandolfo, outside Rome. Every Sunday, at midday, the Pope appears at the window of his study (the second from the right on the top floor of the Apostolic Palace) and makes a speech to the congregation that has gathered in St Peter's Square, followed by the recitation of the *Angelus* (a Catholic prayer on the mystery of Incarnation). The Pope meets the congregation also during general audiences which are held every Wednesday in the Aula Nervi: on these occasions the pope imparts lessons on Catholic doctrine. The Pope also holds official audiences, during which he meets, as head of the Papal State, other heads of State.

Top and bottom, two images of Pope John Paul II. Above right, the emblem of the papacy with the tiara in the centre and the two crossed keys. In the center, the signatures of Pope Benedict XVI and John Paul II with their corresponding coats-of-arms.

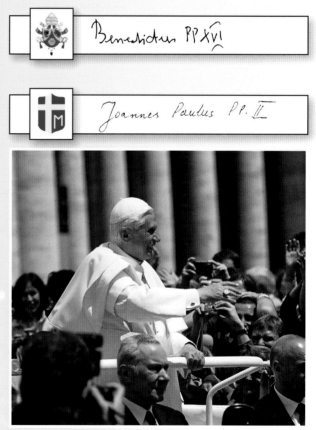

Pope Benedict XVI in the "Popemobile" passing through the crowd gathered in Saint Peter's Square.

John Paul II officiates at a Mass in the Sistine Chapel.

SISTINE CHAPEL

Between 1475 and 1481, under Pope Sixtus IV della Rovere, Giovannino de' Dolci built what may be called the "Chapel of Chapels" to plans by Baccio Pontelli. Architecturally, the Sistine Chapel is a spacious rectangular hall with a barrel vault, divided into two unequal parts by a splendid marble *transenna* or screen by Mino da Fiesole, Giovanni Dalmata and Andrea Bregno. The same artists also made the Cantoria. But the chief attractions of the Sistine Chapel are, of course, its frescoes, particu-

larly those by Michelangelo on the walls and vault. Michelangelo's marvelous paintings postdate those covering the wall facing the altar and the two side walls, painted during the pontificate of Sixtus IV (between 1481 and 1483) by Perugino, Pinturicchio, Luca Signorelli, Cosimo Rosselli, Domenico Ghirlandaio, and Botticelli. At that time the vault was blue and strewn with stars, and so it remained until Julius II commissioned Michelangelo to re-

General view of Michelangelo's ceiling frescoes in the Sistine Chapel. In the center, nine pictures depict the Stories of the Genesis. The twelve frescoes around the vault are of Sibyls and Prophets. Above these figures, softly rendered nudes support festoons and medallions.

MICHELANGELO IN THE SISTINE CHAPEL

Michelangelo, the famed master of the Sistine Chapel, completed his frescoes in two phases: the period between 1508 and 1512 was employed in painting the **vault** under commission by Pope Clement VII, whereas his other masterpiece, the **Last Judgement,** was commissioned by Pope Paul III (Alessandro Farnese) for the back wall of the chapel nearly a quarter of a century later.

These two frescoes, which together cover a surface of approximately 800 square meters, represent perhaps the greatest artistic achievement of all time.

Left, Michelangelo, **Separation of Light from Darkness.**

Bottom, Michelangelo, **Creation of the Sun, Moon and Plants.**
In this painting the artist represents God, seen from behind, pointing to a bush, thus alluding to plant life; on the right, God divides the heaven's orbs, the sun and the moon.

Left, Michelangelo,
Separation of Land and Water.

Above, Michelangelo, **Creation of Adam.**
This is the central scene of the cycle and has its focal point in the contact between the fingers of God and those of Adam, through which the Creator transmits life to man.

Right, Michelangelo,
Creation of Eve.

Bottom, Michelangelo, **Original Sin and Expulsion from Earthly Paradise.** *The scene is divided into two parts by the tree of good and evil, around which coils the serpent offering the apple to Eve, who by accepting it commits the original sin. On the other side the progenitors, bent under the weight of their own shame, are banished from earthly paradise by an angel brandishing a sword.*

Left, Michelangelo, Sacrifice of Noah.

Bottom, Michelangelo, The Flood. *This extremely dramatic scene shows groups of figures about to be engulfed by the waters. In the foreground we see an area of high ground on which people seek refuge and therefore salvation from divine punishment; on the other side figures huddle together on a small island. In the centre a boat is about to sink, while in the background is Noah's ark, Noah's family and the pairs of animals that by God's will are destined to survive the flood.*

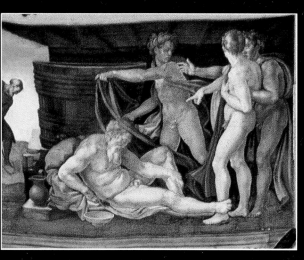

Left, Michelangelo, Drunkenness of Noah.

Right, detail of the north wall. In the lunettes Michelangelo has frescoed the Ancestors of Christ. *Immediately below are four figures in the series of* Popes *that were executed by various artists (Perugino, Sandro Botticelli, Cosimo Rosselli and Domenico Ghirlandaio). In the lower fascia are two frescoes from the cycle representing* Scenes from the Life of Christ: The Consignment of the Keys *by Perugino and the* Last Supper *by Cosimo Rosselli. Below each of these panels are false draperies with the emblems of Sixtus IV.*

South wall, Sandro Botticelli, **Scenes from the Life of Moses.** *This fresco is part of the* **Life of Moses** *cycle.*

Back wall, Michelangelo, **Last Judgement** *(overall view). Twenty-five years after the frescoing of the vault, between 1536 and 1541, Michelangelo painted this large new fresco, which covers the whole of the wall. Its enormous size made necessary the destruction of two Peruginesque frescoes and the filling in of two of the large arched windows.*

South wall, Perugino, **Journey of Moses into Egypt.**

The 18th-century facade of the basilica.
Below, the arched loggia set against the facade and the mosaics
that decorate it, executed by Filippo Rusuti (late 13th century).

The basilicas

BASILICA OF SANTA MARIA MAGGIORE

In August of 352 AD, snow miraculously fell on the Esquiline hill, and in it Pope Liberius traced the perimeter of the first church on the site, popularly called *Santa Maria della Neve* (Our Lady of the Snow). The present Basilica of Santa Maria Maggiore was completely rebuilt by Sixtus III (432-440). The basilica was neither restored nor rebuilt until the 12th century, when Eugene III had a portico built for the facade, much like those still standing in San Lorenzo fuori le Mura or in San Giorgio al Velabro. At the end of the 13th century, Nicholas IV promoted the renovation of the apse. Only in the 18th century did Clement XII, after having demolished the old portico, entrust the creation of a new facade to Ferdinando Fuga. Now giving the impression of being squeezed between the two tall flanking buildings (dating to the 17th and 18th centu-

Santa Maria Maggiore: the cupola of the Sistine Chapel.

ries), the **facade** is preceded by a vast flight of steps and features a portico with an architrave on the ground floor and a loggia with arches above; the whole is crowned by a balustrade which curiously extends on either side of the facade to define the twin palaces at the sides. Rich sculptural decoration runs along the front and under the portico, while the loggia of the upper

Below right, the Nativity scene built by Arnolfo di Cambio and today visible in the museum of the basilica. It is the earliest representation of its kind made with statues.

TO VISIT

Basilica of San Giovanni in Laterano p. 104
Basilica of San Lorenzo fuori le Mura p. 111
Basilica of San Paolo fuori le Mura p. 108
Basilica of San Pietro in Vincoli p. 103
Basilica of Santa Croce in Gerusalemme p. 107
Basilica of Santa Maria Maggiore p. 101
Church of Santa Maria in Trastevere p. 113
Domus Aurea p. 102
Trastevere p. 113

MUSEUM OF THE BASILICA OF SANTA MARIA MAGGIORE

The museum was inaugurated on 8 December 2001 by Pope John Paul II. Displayed in it are the most precious objects belonging to the basilica: books, monstrances, chalices, paintings and liturgical vestments. Very interesting are some old musical scores belonging to the Music Chapel.

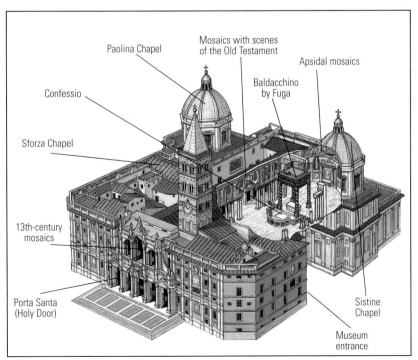

Paolina Chapel
Mosaics with scenes of the Old Testament
Apsidal mosaics
Baldacchino by Fuga
Confessio
Sforza Chapel
13th-century mosaics
Porta Santa (Holy Door)
Sistine Chapel
Museum entrance

In the Pauline Chapel is the icon of the "Salus Populi Romani", which according to tradition was painted by Luke the evangelist.

Nero's Domus Aurea in a fanciful 17th-century reconstruction.

DOMUS AUREA

The magnificent residence that Nero built after the great fire that destroyed Rome in 64 AD extended over an area of 80 hectares, that is, nearly the entire center of Rome. All that remains today of the lavish palace is 150 rooms of the portion on Colle Oppio. The most important and striking rooms include the **nymphaeum** with the mosaic of *Ulysses Offering a Cup of Wine to Polyphemus*, the **room with the golden ceiling**, the **room of Hector and Andromache**, the **room of Achilles at Skyros** and the **Octagonal Room**.

The grandiose interior of the Basilica.

floor (13th century) still preserves the mosaic decoration of the older facade. The **interior** is on a tripartite basilica plan with forty Ionic columns supporting an entablature with a mosaic frieze. The coffered *ceiling* is commonly attributed to Giuliano da Sangallo, while, the pavement is in Cosmatesque marblework, although much of it was restored under Benedict XIV.

The mosaic of the Coronation of the Virgin *(13th cent.) in the apse.*

Basilica of San Pietro in Vincoli: Michelangelo's tomb of Julius II with the statue of Moses at the center. At the sides, left, the statue of Rachel (personifying the "contemplative life"); right, Leah ("active life").

> *"And it came to pass, when Moses came down from Mount Sinai . . . Moses wist not that the skin of his face shone while he talked with Him."*
> (Exodus 34:29)

Moses, prophet and leader of the Jews during the exodus from ancient Egypt to the promised land, is portrayed by Michelangelo as he severely regards the idolatrous Jews while holding in his right hand the Tables of the Law received on Mount Sinai. The two small horns over his head allude to the light which, according to the Bible story, shone from his forehead after the divine revelation.

BASILICA OF SAN PIETRO IN VINCOLI

This is without doubt one of the most venerated minor basilicas in Rome, rich as it is in the memory of the first Pope of the Church, from whom it received its name. It is also called the Basilica Eudoxiana, after the wife of emperor Valentinian III. Eudoxiana, upon receiving from her mother the chains that had bound Saint Peter during his imprisonment in Jerusalem, donated them to Pope Saint Leo I. When the Pope set these chains with the ones that had bound the wrists and ankles of Saint Peter in the Mamertine Prison, he saw the two **chains** unite to form a single piece. This relic is still kept here and the old Latin name of church, '*in vinculis*', has remained. In the right transept is the major attraction of the church, the unfinished **Mausoleum of Julius II** by Michelangelo with the imposing figure of Michelangelo's *Moses* in the center.

Basilica of San Pietro in Vincoli: Michelangelo, Moses.

CLEMENS·XII·PONT·MAX·ANNO·V   CHRISTO·SALVATORI   IN·HON·SS·IOAN·BAPT·ET·EVANG

The main facade of the Basilica of San Giovanni in Laterano.

One of the twelve statues of Apostles that line the nave.

BAPTISTERY OF SAINT JOHN

Originally raised by Constantine, the baptistery was completely reconstructed a number of times; the building we see today dates to the 17th century. It is also known as San Giovanni in Fonte or in Laterano. The structure is that of the prototype Christian baptistery.

BASILICA OF SAN GIOVANNI IN LATERANO

Originally built by Constantine, plundered by the Genseric's Vandals, frequently sacked, damaged by the earthquake of 896 and various fires–for most of its existence, the Basilica of San Giovanni in Laterano has been the object of reconstruction and restoration. The balustrade above the attic supports the colossal statues of *Christ, Saints John the Baptist and John the Evangelist*, and the *Doctors of the Church*. There are five entrances (the last to the right is known as the *"Porta Santa"* and is opened only in Jubilee years), each surmounted by a loggia. The *statue of Emperor Constantine* was brought here from the Baths of Diocletian. The majestic **interior** is a Latin cross with a nave and two aisles on either side. The great conch of the apse at the back of the basilica is covered with *mosaics* dating to the 4th, 6th, and 13th centuries (note, in particular, the figures of the *Apostles* signed by Jacopo Torriti). Above the organ, a large 19th-century fresco by Francesco Grandi depicts episodes concerning the *Founding and Construction of the Basilica*. The decoration of the transept also deals with analogous subjects; it was completely restored during the pontificate of Clement VIII by the architect Giovanni Della Porta and the painter known as the Cavalier d'Arpino. Under the Cavalier d'Arpino's fresco of the *Ascension of Christ* is the gilded bronze pediment, supported by antique bronze columns, that protects the *altar of the Chapel of the Holy Sacrament* designed for Clement VIII by Pietro Paolo Olivieri and supporting a precious ciborium. Among the many other chapels built in various periods as further decoration for the basilica are the **Colonna Chapel**, also know as the **Choir Chapel**, by Girolamo Rainaldi (1625); the **Chapel of the Crucifixion**, which preserves a fragment of the presumed *funeral monument of Nicholas IV* attributed to Adeodato di Cosma (13th century); the **Chapel of Massimo**, by Giacomo Della Porta; the **Torlonia Chapel**, quite different from that preceding it and splendidly decorated in neo-Renaissance style by the architect Raimondi (1850); and the architecturally-complete and self-sufficient **Corsini Chapel**, built on the Greek-cross plan by Alessandro Galilei for Clement XII. A corridor leads to the **Old Sacristy**, with the *Annunciation* by Venuti and a *Saint John the Evangelist* by the Cavalier d'Arpino, and to the **New Sacristy**, with a 15th-century *Annunciation* of the Tuscan school. In the nearby Cosmatesque **Cloister**, a 13th-century work by Vassalletto, are visible remains of the most ancient portion of the basilica.

Interior of the Basilica of San Giovanni in Laterano with its fine Cosmatesque pavement.

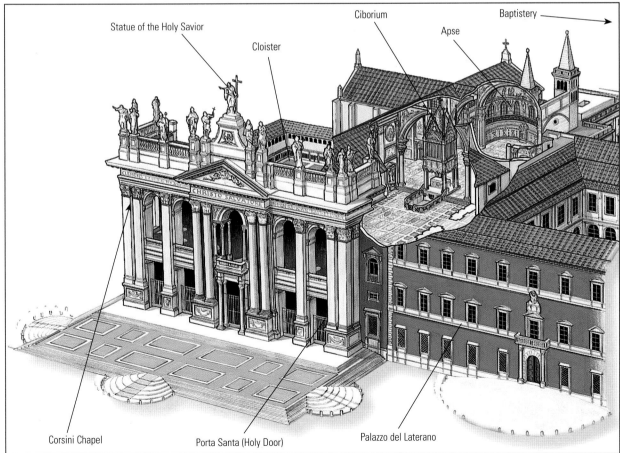

Statue of the Holy Savior

Cloister

Ciborium

Apse

Baptistery

Corsini Chapel

Porta Santa (Holy Door)

Palazzo del Laterano

SCALA SANTA

The Palazzo del Sancta Sanctorum owes its name to the fact that was originally designed to contain, or incorporate, the Popes' Chapel (or *Sancta Sanctorum*). Pope Sixtus V commissioned the palace from the architect Domenico Fontana, who built it in 1585-1590. The chapel was originally part of a building known as the "Patriarchio" (7th - 8th centuries) that at the time housed the papal court. The name of "Scala Santa" derives from the erroneous identification of one of the staircases of the Patriarchio as the flight of stairs in Pilate's *Praetorium* ascended by Christ when he was judged by Pilate. Nowadays, the term *Sancta Sanctorum* is used to indicate the **Chapel of Saint Laurence**, overflowing with relics and at the same time a true jewel of Cosmatesque art with its tabernacles along the walls and its mosaic ceiling.

The Scala Santa.

The Gothic baldachin (14th century) decorated with frescoes surmounting the papal altar, thus called because it can be used only by the Pope to celebrate Mass.

BASILICA OF SANTA CROCE IN GERUSALEMME

Santa Croce di Gerusalemme has been known since the Middle Ages as the 'basilica of the relics' due to the great number of mementos of saints and martyrs it contains. Its official name derives from the soil of the Holy Sepulcher in Jerusalem brought here by Saint Helena. The **interior** is significant with its beautiful wooden *ceiling*. To the right of the apse, the **Chapel of Saint Helena**, founded by contains the soil of the Holy Sepulcher under its floor; the *mosaic* that adorns the upper portion of the walls and the vault is a Renaissance work variously attributed to Melozzo da Forlì and Baldassare Peruzzi. Of inestimable religious value is the **Chapel of the Relics**, containing the fragments of the True Cross, the Holy Thorns of Christ's Crown, and other significant sacred relics.

Santa Croce in Gerusalemme: interior with the 18th-century baldachin.

Detail of the facade of Santa Croce in Gerusalemme.

The facade and the quadriporticus of the Basilica of San Paolo fuori le Mura.

BASILICA OF SAN PAOLO FUORI LE MURA

Built by Constantine over the tomb of the apostle Paul, the church remained standing until 15 July 1823, when it was gutted by fire. It was not reconsecrated until 1854. The **facade** rising above the quadriporticus is richly decorated with mosaics both in the gable (the *Blessing Christ with Saints Peter and Paul*) and in the frieze (an *Agnus Dei* on a hill that rises up symbolically between the two holy cities of Jerusalem and Bethlehem), and with the four large *Symbols of the Prophets* alternating with the three windows.

In the **interior** two stately statues of *Saint Peter and Saint Paul* overlook the raised transept with the sumptuous triumphal arch dating to the time of Leo the Great, called the *Arch of Galla Placidia*, which frames the apse and which was already decorated with mosaics in the 5th century. In the 13th century the mosaics were replaced by Honorius III, who employed Venetian craftsmen sent for the purpose to the pope by the doge of Venice. Objects housed in the Basilica include the Gothic *ciborium* made by Arnolfo di Cambio in 1285 in collaboration with a certain "Petro" who some believe to have been Pietro Cavallini, the equally presumed author of the *mosaics* (of which only fragments remain) now decorating the reverse side of the arch of triumph and once part of the decoration of the exterior of the Basilica.

Under the exquisite canopy of Arnolfo's tabernacle is the altar over the *tomb of Saint Paul* with the inevitable *fenestrella confessionis* (confessional window) through which can be seen the 4th-century epigraph reading "Paulo Apostolo Mart."

A detail of the mosaic of the facade with the blessing Christ.

The large mosaic of the apse with the blessing Christ, *the work of Venetian artists.*

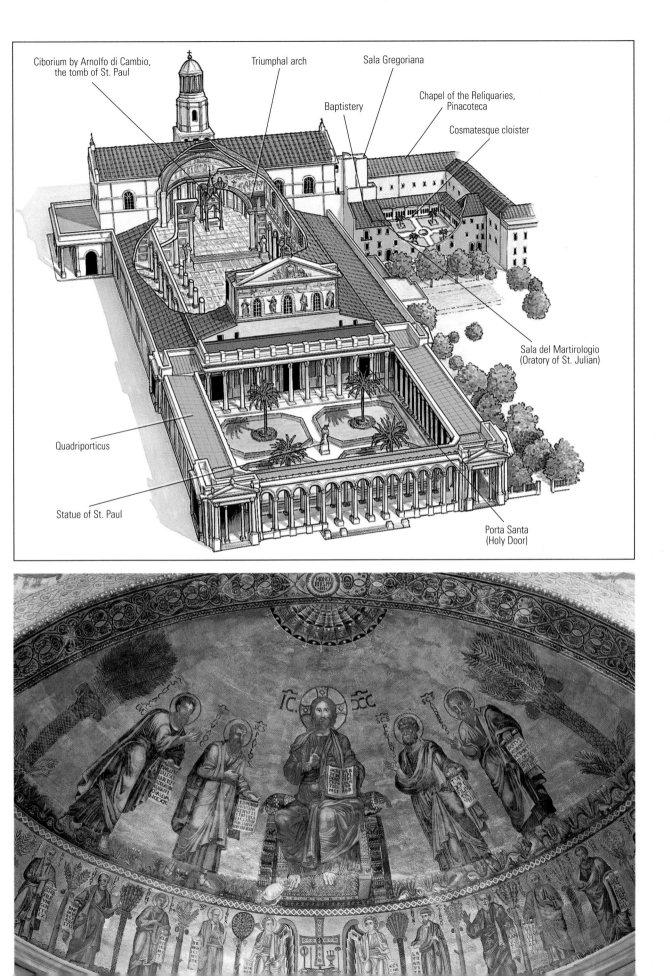

Ciborium by Arnolfo di Cambio, the tomb of St. Paul

Triumphal arch

Sala Gregoriana

Baptistery

Chapel of the Reliquaries, Pinacoteca

Cosmatesque cloister

Sala del Martirologio (Oratory of St. Julian)

Quadriporticus

Statue of St. Paul

Porta Santa (Holy Door)

A view of the interior.

A detail of the splendid coffered ceiling.

Bottom, the space beneath the altar
housing the tomb of St. Paul.

Inside San Paolo fuori le Mura is an
unusual mosaic frieze that also runs
in the side aisles. Represented in it are
portraits of the popes in the long history
of the Catholoic church, from Saint
Peter to the present day.

The basilicas

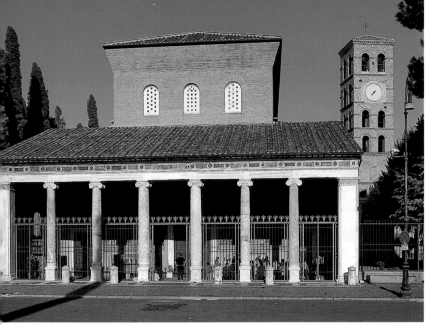

The 13-century portico of San Lorenzo fuori le Mura.

BASILICA OF SAN LORENZO FUORI LE MURA

San Lorenzo arose from the fusion of the Pelagian Basilica, dedicated to Saint Lawrence, and Honorius' church dedicated to the Virgin, commissioned by the popes Pelagius II (6th century) and Honorius III (13th century), respectively. The lovely **portico** dates to the 13th century. Alongside are the monastery, with its beautiful **cloister**, and the late 12th-century Romanesque **bell tower**. The **interior** shows evident signs of the origin of the building as the fusion of two churches that while contiguous were laid out on different axes.

The romanesque bell tower of the Basilica.

A view of the cloister.

CHURCH OF SANTA MARIA IN TRASTEVERE

Possibly founded around 221 AD by Saint Calixtus (or so at least legend would have it), the church was completely rebuilt at the dawn of the second millennium and again restructured in the 18th century by Pope Clement XI. In the apse, at the height of the windows, are various outstanding **mosaics** by Cavallini narrating *Scenes from the Life of the Virgin*.

The exterior (bottom), a detail of the upper portion of the facade (left) and a view of the interior (bottom left) of the Church of Santa Maria in Trastevere.

Above, two images of the picturesque trattorie of Trastevere and a view of Piazzetta Trilussa.

di Porta Portese piazza

TRASTEVERE

Trastevere has always been considered a working-class district. From the time of the Republic it was inhabited by Jewish and Syrian immigrants and artisans, small traders, sailors, and fishermen attracted by the proximity of the Tiber river port. In the Middle Ages, Trastevere acquired new streets and lanes that remain the characteristic cornice for churches of great artistic value. Today, enlivened by trattorie, pubs, charming small shops, and markets, the district has made a name for itself as one of the capital's liveliest, day and night.

An aerial view of Porta San Paolo and the Pyramid of Caius Cestius enclosed in the Aurelian Walls.

Two views of the Baths of Caracalla.

Aventine

PORTA SAN PAOLO AND THE PYRAMID OF CAIUS CESTIUS

What is now known as Porta San Paolo is one of the best preserved of Rome's city gates (the other is Porta San Sebastiano) in the formidable circuit of the **Aurelian Walls**. The rooms inside the building now house the **Museo della Via Ostiense**. A curious funeral monument of the early Imperial period, the **Pyramid of Caius Cestius**, was raised next to *Porta Ostiensis* during the construction of the Aurelian walls. The building was obviously inspired by Egyptian models, of the Ptolemaic period rather than that of the pharaohs, as was fashionable in Rome after the conquest of Egypt in 30 BC.

Caracalla

BATHS OF CARACALLA

The Baths of Caracalla are a magnificent, and excellently-preserved, example of *thermae* from the Imperial period. Construction was begun by the emperor Caracalla in 212 AD. The baths continued to function until 537 when, during the siege of Rome by Vitiges and his Goths, the aqueducts of the city were cut off. In the 16th century, excavations carried out in the enormous building brought to light various works of art including the *Farnese Bull* and the *Hercules*, now in the National Museum of Naples. The *mosaics of athletes* that decorated the hemicycles of the large side courtyards of the *thermae* were discovered in 1824 (now in the Vatican Museums).

Appia Antica

VIA APPIA ANTICA

The most important of the Roman consular roads, known as the *Regina Viarum* (the queen of roads), begins at Porta San Sebastiano and winds towards the interior bordered with ancient and not-so-ancient monuments. Miraculous events such as the famous episode of "Domine quo vadis?" are thought to have taken place along this thoroughfare.

CHURCH OF "DOMINE QUO VADIS?"

The church known by this famous phrase actually seems to have been dedicated to *Santa Maria in Palmis*. But the worldwide fame of the building rests less on its artistic merits than on Christian tradition, which relates that the site on which the church stands was the spot where Jesus appeared to Peter as he was fleeing Rome for fear of being crucified. The apostle, taken aback, uttered the famous phrase *Domine quo vadis?* ("Lord, where are you going?"); Jesus is said to have answered *"Venio iterum crucifigi"* ("I am returning to be crucified"). Peter grasped the implicit invitation in Christ's words and returned to Rome and martyrdom.

Panorama of the Via Appia with the Tomb of Cecilia Metella in the background.

TO VISIT

Basilica of San Sebastiano p. 118
Catacomb of Domitilla p. 117
Catacomb of Saint Calixtus p. 116
Church of
 "Domine quo vadis?" p. 115
EUR p. 119
Tomb of Cecilia Metella p. 119
Via Appia Antica p. 115

The simple facade of the Church of "Domine Quo Vadis?".

Below, Porta San Sebastiano and the stone paving of the Via Appia Antica.

CATACOMBS OF ST. CALIXTUS

These vast catacombs, spreading out over four levels with some 20 kilometers of galleries, display an immense number of *cubicula* and *hypogea* decorated with frescoes in the preserved areas. The most ancient nucleus are the **Papal Crypt**, where the popes who were martyred and sanctified in the first centuries of Christianity were buried; the **Crypt of St. Cecilia**, where the body of the young martyr was found; the **Crypt of Lucina;** and the **Cubicula of the Sacraments**, with 3rd-century frescoes representing a wide range of religious objects. Dating from the 4th century are the **Crypts of Saints Gaius and Eusebius**, with the *sarcophagi* of the two popes.

Catacombs of Saint Calixtus: the painting of the Good Shepherd *in the Crypt of Lucina and a view of the Crypt of Santa Cecilia.*

Catacombs of Domitilla: the Basilica of the Saints Nereus and Achilleus and a section of the galleries.

CATACOMBS OF DOMITILLA

The catacombs, also called the Catacombs of Saints Nereus and Achilleus, are among the largest in Rome. According to tradition, they were built from the simple household sepulcher that belonged to Domitilla, the wife and niece of Flavius Clement and put to death by Domitian.

Inside of the catacombs are the remains of the **Basilica dei Santi Nereo e Achilleo**: behind the apse is a cubiculum containing the fresco of *The defunct venerable invoking St. Petronilla*. Near the basilica is the very ancient *Cemetery of the Flavians*. In another area of the catacombs is the so-called 'Good Shepherd', which takes its name from a sculpture and which preserves 2nd-century AD paintings in the vault. Found in a later area are fine depictions of the grain market and scenes of everyday work (3rd-4th century).

BASILICA OF SAN SEBASTIANO

Built as the *Basilica Apostolorum* where the bodies of Saints Paul and Peter were once kept temporarily, the church, one of the seven pilgrimage churches of Rome, was dedicated to St. Sebastian in the middle of the 4th century. In the early 1600s, Cardinal Scipione Borghese asked Flaminio Ponzio to rebuild the church, giving it an elegant **facade** with a portico and an **interior** with a single nave and a fine wooden ceiling.

CATACOMBS OF SAN SEBASTIANO

Dug out of an ancient stone quarry, the catacombs of St. Sebastian were initially a pagan burial grounds before being used by Christians. They were actually composed of three **Mausoleums**, built in the 2nd century and covered with earth a century later to create an open flat area, the so-called **Triclia**, with a portico where the *refrigeria*, or liturgical banquets, were held and where the relics of Saints Peter and Paul, brought here temporarily in 258, were worshipped. The central focus of the intricate labyrinth of galleries is the **Crypt of St. Sebastian**, where the martyr who gave his name to the entire burial grounds was entombed. The numerous rooms of the catacombs have extremely interesting frescoes. Worthy of note among them is the fresco in the **Cubiculum of Jonah**, with a cycle depicting the famous biblical figure, and the *Miracle of the demoniac of Gerasa*, preserved in one of the three mausoleums. The subterranean grounds also contain the remains of the **Basilica Apostolorum**.

Above, the facade of the Basilica of San Sebastiano.

Basilica of San Sebastiano: detail of the wooden ceiling with the image of the martyrdom of St. Sebastian and a view of the interior.

View of the Tomb of Cecilia Metella, symbol of the Via Appia Antica.

TOMB OF CECILIA METELLA

This sumptuous and typically Roman mausoleum was originally built in the late Republican period for Cecilia, the wife of Crassus and daughter of Quintus Metellus, the conqueror of Crete. It was modified in 1302 by the Caetani family, who adapted it to perform defensive functions for their neighboring castle. Even so, the cella of the ancient tomb, with its conical covering, can still identified.

View of the interior of the Tomb of Cecilia Metella.

Three suggestive views of the 20th-century Palazzo della Civiltà del Lavoro.

EUR

This famous district, at one and the same time among the most recent and the most historical, was originally conceived as the site of the Esposizione Universale di Roma that was scheduled to have been held in 1942. Designed by a group of famous architects (Pagano, Piccinato, Vietti and Rossi) coordinated and directed by Marcello Piacentini, it covers an area of 420 hectares in the shape of a pentagon. The formative concept was that of monumentality, and the district was developed with a view to the future expansion of Rome toward the Tyrrhenian Sea. Among the significant paradigms of Italian architecture of the first half of the 20th century are the **Palazzo della Civiltà del Lavoro** and the buildings housing the **Museo Preistorico-Etnografico Pigorini**, the **Museo dell'Alto Medioevo**, the **Museo delle Arti e Tradizioni Popolari**, and the **Museo della Civiltà Romana**. Opening soon in this historic district, the new **Centro Congressi** Italia convention center on an area of 27,000 square meters. The plans, by architect Massimiliano Fuksas, call for innovative logistics solutions for the complex and use of high-tech construction materials.

IMPERIAL FORUMS ▪ **ROMAN FORUM** ▪ **PALATINE HILL** ▪ **CAPITOLINE HILL**

IMPERIAL FORUMS

Temple of Divus Trajanus
Trajan's Column
Basilica Ulpia
Trajan's Markets
Trajan's Forum
Forum of Augustus
Temple of Mars Ultor
Temple of Venus Genitrix
Caesar's Forum
Nerva's Forum
  or Forun Transitorium
Forum of Peace

ROMAN FORUM AND COLOSSEUM

Temple of Saturn
Arch of Septimius Severus
Basilica Julia
Temple of Augustus
Temple of Castor and Pollux
Curia
Basilica Aemilia
Temple of Antoninus and Faustina
Temple of Divus Julius
Temple of Vesta
House of the Vestals
Basilica of Maxentius
Temple of Venus and Rome
Arch of Titus
Arch of Constantine
Colosseum

PALATINE HILL AND CIRCUS MAXIMUS

Circus Maximus
Domus Augustana
Domus Flavia

CAPITOLINE HILL

Temple of Jupiter
Temple of Juno Moneta
Temple of Virtus

© Copyright
by Casa Editrice Bonechi, via Cairoli 18/b, Firenze - Italia
E-mail: bonechi@bonechi.it

Concept and project: Casa Editrice Bonechi. *Editorial management:* Monica Bonechi. *Graphic design and cover:* Manuela Ranfagni. *Texts compiled by the* Casa Editrice Bonechi Editorial Department. *Editing:* Elena Rossi. *Drawings:* Sauro Giampaia (p. 23), Stefano Benini (pp. 101, 105, 109, inside front and back covers).

Printed in Italy by Centro Stampa Editoriale Bonechi - Sesto Fiorentino.

The photographs in this book are the property of the Casa Editrice Bonechi Archives *and were taken by* Marco Bonechi *and* Paolo Giambone; Gaetano Barone *(p. 86)*,
Maria Novella Batini *(pp. 44, left, 45 bottom right, 46 top and bottom left, 113 right)*, Gianni Dagli Orti *(pp. 35 bottom, 69 bottom right, 70 bottom left)*,
Francesco Giannoni *(pp. 9 right, 57 top left, 66 bottom, 67 bottom, 71 bottom, 87 top, 119 top right)*, Giuliano Valsecchi *(p. 11 bottom left)*.
The photographs on pp. 90 (left) and 91, belonging to the archive of Casa Editrice Bonechi, were supplied by Arturo Mari, Osservatore Romano.
The following photographers also contributed to this publication: Adnkronos: *p. 84 bottom*; Archivio Fabbrica di San Pietro: *pp. 80, 81, 82 left*; Foto Pont. Comm. Arch. Sacra: *pp. 116, 117*;
© Foto Scala, Firenze: *pp. 35 top* (© 2005, Ann Rohan/HIP/Scala, Firenze*), 57 top right* (© 2006, Foto Scala, Firenze/Luciano Romano) *and bottom right* (© 2008, Foto Scala, Firenze – by courtesy
of Ministero dei Beni e Attività Culturali), 119 *bottom left* (© 1990, Foto Scala, Firenze); Andrea Jemolo: *pp. 10 left, 50 bottom right, 53 bottom left, 58 top, 60 top, 60-61, 62 top and bottom left, 64
bottom, 73 bottom, 87 bottom, 103 top*; Marka: *p. 124 top* (© Javier Larrea); Musei Vaticani: *pp. 1 right, 92-93, 94, 95, 96, 97* (A. Bracchetti, P. Zigrossi), 98 *top* (A. Bracchetti, P. Zigrossi),
98 *bottom* (P. Zigrossi), 99, 121-123, *photo of the "Creation of Adam" by Michelangelo on the left flap*; Ghigo Roli: *pp. 3, 11 top, 20-21, 28 top*; Simephoto: *pp. 22, 34 right, 40-41 top, 47 top,
48, 50 top, 54, 55 bottom, 59 bottom, 63 top left, 83, 90 bottom right, 115 bottom left and bottom right, front cover (second photo in the centre)*; Arnaldo Vescovo: *pp. 66 in top, 67 top.*

The publisher apologizes for any unintentional omissions, and would be pleased to include appropriate acknowledgements in any subsequent edition of this publication.

ISBN 978-88-476-2445-0
www.bonechi.com

A 10 9 8 7 6 5 4 3 2 1